keeping a calm center

Born of adversity during the first weeks of the CO-VID-19 pandemic, this series of reflections was offered as a virtual embrace to the members of Sacred Journeys Spiritual Community. Addressing the collective sighs of loss, disruption, isolation, and despair, Pastor Kaye began issuing these daily messages to offer counsel and comfort, contemplation and connection… a reminder of the grace of community.

Refreshingly straightforward, the reflections expose the poetry in the mundane. They point to spiritual truths and insights that paradoxically offer us opportunities for fuller growth while experiencing new and formidable obstacles. The essence of this collection encourages us to listen to the ever-present guidance of the divine voice within and around us, to surrender to our authentic selves, embrace the mystery, and fully engage with a spirituality of abundance. A heartwarming and uplifting collection for all souls, not just those burdened by the pandemic.

~ Scott Mandernack, Associate Dean for Scholarly Resources and Collections at Marquette University

Fear, uncertainty, and isolation! Suddenly and almost without warning, our smaller, close-knit spiritual community was forced into a situation not unlike so many others, where we were unable to meet in person. To a community so used to the physical presence of others, the question became this: how do we encourage, uplift, and provide a regular source of hope and connection while recognizing the difficult unknown we were all facing? Our pastor, Kaye Glennon, began sending emails each morning offering hope, courage, peace, wisdom, understanding, and so much more, but most importantly, a way to connect. This book is the end result of these daily offerings. They are not limited to COVID-like situations. They are available to anyone who seeks comfort, encouragement, understanding, and other pathways to connect with the Divine.

~ Susan McClintock Perry, President, Board of Directors, Sacred Journeys Spiritual Community

Keeping a Calm Center is a gift. Receive it; embrace its wisdom; be embraced by its compassion; and then give it away again. Remember, the center is always coming full circle. Read this book. Let it unscramble your soul, then sigh and breathe deep, and take a step down the road less traveled. Kaye Glennon is an excellent spiritual leader and writer, and she knows the way home to a soul at peace. Follow my advice, and follow Kaye's. You won't regret it.

~ Rev. Bill Grimbol, pastor and author of "Let Grace Be Your Guide"

Kaye Glennon shares personal experiences which allow a connection to one's own life experiences with new perspectives for growth and oneness with the Divine. Challenging each person to go deeper into self-awareness, this collection of thought-provoking reflections helps one to live in the moment with courage and gratitude, so each can become their authentic self.

~ Robin Smerchek, Retired Power Generation Director of Engineering at We Energies

Kaye Glennon's collection of reflections helps us find our true selves. Her writings guide us inward toward self-love and connection with the divine, leading us out of the dark forest to the light of hope.

~ Sally Nuciforo, retired nurse

Pastor Kaye is held in many hearts of her congregation as their mother. In this time of adversity, she challenges her children to find courage with her as their companion.

~ Barbara Hammes, former hospice coordinator

keeping a calm center

KAYE GLENNON

Ten|16 PRESS

www.ten16press.com - Waukesha, WI

www.ten16press.com
Waukesha, WI

Cover Designer: Faith Smith
Art Director: Kaeley Dunteman
Photography: Bryn Glennon

*Helping someone believe in themself
is the greatest superpower ever.
To all those who believed in me,
I am more grateful
than you will ever know.*

TABLE OF CONTENTS

FOREWORD

2020 was one wild ride of a year. At times, it felt like trying to jog during an earthquake, and at other times, well, it took me back to my first adolescent drinking binge, when the spinning just would not stop. However, this time I had nothing to throw up, except maybe a very scrambled soul.

During this past year, I drew great comfort and purpose from the ministry of Kaye Glennon, spiritual leader of a fine group of progressive folks, the spiritual community of Sacred Journeys in Racine, Wisconsin. Kaye knew her flock was hurting, adrift, lonely, and confused. She made a very smart decision. She wrote to us daily for several months.

Her messages, like her preaching and teaching and person, were direct, candid, practical, funny, empathetic, and above all else, nourishing for the soul. It made a difference for many of us. It helped!

As a fellow writer and pastor, I encouraged Kaye to rewrite these messages for a wider audience, as I felt strongly that they could be a real shot in the heart for anyone who read them. I still believe this to be true, and after helping edit the revised manuscript, I am convinced Kaye has written something disarmingly simple, but so very on point, and such a spiritual boost. Kaye's writing is clear, and the messages are not meant to dazzle us with theological insights, but rather are intended to bring us home to a soul looking for hope.

The pandemic has been frightening and will be for quite some time. This experience is so new to us, and there has been such a void of leadership. The state of our culture has been equally upsetting. The divisions among us have reached abyssal depth, and there is so much anger and frustration in the air. I think we have hit a real spiritual bottom as a society, and whether or not my assessment is correct, Kaye's thoughtful book offers a big dose of positive and productive energy.

I believe we are all in need of a return to a spiritual foundation. This is exactly what you will find in *Keeping a Calm Center*. Kaye writes to her readers as a friend, a neighbor, a fellow traveler on the journey of faith, and she is wise enough not to offer a map, but she makes excellent suggestions about when and where to stop along the way. She gently reminds us how much we need the solitude, silence and stillness, and ironically, the community, a gathering of Grace, and the climb together up to higher ground.

As a woman, a friend, a neighbor, a pastor, and now a fine writer, Kaye offers us a voice of genuine compassion, care, concern, courage, and creativity. She is a good guide at a time when we are feeling lost on almost a daily basis. Spiritually, Kaye is superb at bringing us home. Home, where we belong, we fit, we are understood, we have a point and a purpose, our stories matter, and we can trust one another.

Keeping a Calm Center reminded me how when we are lost, we must have faith that we will be found, and when someone we love is lost, we must go out and look for them. This isn't rocket science; it is the real good life in action. Kaye has written a really good book, one which seeks to go out and find us, and in the pages of this lovely work, we will feel the gracious touch of her hand and heart, as she helps us get back home to our own souls.

She does not claim to know the whole way, but she has wonderful ideas about the direction, and this is always the best beginning. The first step is the toughest and the most important. The right direction is the prerequisite of all hope.

—Rev. William R. Grimbol

INTRODUCTION

In my life, I can't remember another time when we, as a country, have felt more troubled, more disconnected, more divided, more stressed, more scared, more frustrated, and more lost. It didn't feel this way with the AIDS crisis, or after 9/11, or even after the market crashed in 2008. What people express to me is that they are physically, mentally, and spiritually exhausted. They are unmotivated, depressed, anxious, and worried. And it's no wonder. Not only have we been dealing with the COVID-19 pandemic, but also with a radically divided and divisive political scene, and an escalating racial crisis.

Unlike other crises where people band together to see each other through, this pandemic has demanded that we social-distance and isolate from one another. The command to "social-distance" may have been the biggest mistake of this health crisis. Instead, we should have been encouraged to physically distance but socially connect. Our souls desperately need each other for comfort, strength, love, laughter, and support. This has never been more obvious.

Merry-go-rounds were a childhood favorite of mine, back when I didn't get sick spinning in circles. It was exciting to jump on and grab hold, hair blowing wildly, laughter bubbling up, clinging to the metal bars as tightly as our small hands could hold. Eventually, the pusher got tired or fell down from going too fast, and we could tumble off, flopping to the ground to catch our breath and waiting for the world to stop moving.

These days, it feels like we're on a merry-go-round that someone is pushing faster and faster, and we are slipping farther and farther toward the edge. Many of us are barely hanging on by our fingernails for dear life. There is an inescapable fear that if we lose our grip and tumble off, we'll either be trampled by the forces that are spinning us or get sucked under that viciously twirling metal circle and befall a worse fate. What we've almost forgotten is that if we could make our way to the middle of the merry-go-round and anchor ourselves firmly in that center, we could spin forever without being tossed about or thrown off. There is calm in the center. This is what I wanted to provide for people during the chaotic merry-go-round ride that was 2020: a calm center to begin each day.

Every day for about five months, I shared my life, struggles, insecurities, stories, thoughts, and theology. I hoped to help people really think about what was happening, not just "out there" but also within themselves. I hoped to be a friend and a spiritual voice they could count on. I hoped that my voice could ease their anxieties, deepen their spirituality, offer hope, give them a chuckle now and then, and remind them that they aren't alone. We were all trying to hang on as best we could and were dealing with a wide variety of feelings and emotions about it all . . . sometimes all in one day! I hoped that together we would laugh and cry, whine and celebrate, pray and wonder, worry and surrender.

While these reflections were written during a specific crisis, I believe the experiences translate to any time we struggle to make sense of life, ourselves, and the One who connects us all. May they ground you, feed you, comfort you, bring you hope, connect you to your Source, and keep you from falling off that tornado of a merry-go-round.

Love & Light!
Kaye

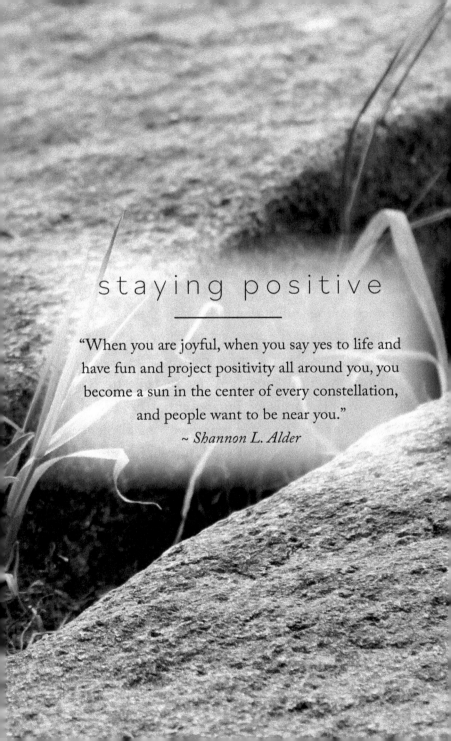

staying positive

———————

"When you are joyful, when you say yes to life and
have fun and project positivity all around you, you
become a sun in the center of every constellation,
and people want to be near you."
~ *Shannon L. Alder*

CHANGE THE QUESTIONS

I was raised by a master questioner, so I'm really good at asking questions. This has not always been seen as a positive thing. My high school friends sometimes referred to me as the "interrogator" for my questioning ability when they brought new dates around. I was just trying to get to know them, but I suppose it is all about your perspective.

Don't worry, I didn't restrict my questioning skills to only unsuspecting potential boyfriends and girlfriends. Over the years, I've asked plenty of questions of myself, of God, of religion and of other people. Along the way, I've learned that what we ask makes a difference in how we live. Believe it or not, we have the ability to change our lives by changing the questions we ask.

For example, you may not have this problem, but I'm prone to questioning the decisions I've made or the things that I've done. I can barrage myself with questions like: *Why did I do that? Why didn't I respond differently? What would have happened if I'd gone left instead of right? Did I do the right thing?*

I can get stuck in this never-ending loop of critical, self-doubting questions when what's done is done. I can't edit the past, sadly. But I can move forward more positively. Doing this requires new questions: *What did I learn from that situation? What is my next best step? What would Love have me do now? How can I make lemonade from the lemons I just picked?*

Here are a few more ideas. Instead of asking what we did wrong today, we can ask what we did right. Instead of asking what won't work about an idea, we could ask how we can make it work. Instead of asking why we can't accomplish something, we could ask what we need to do in order to accomplish the task. Our questions function like the balance beam of a tightrope walker – they help us move forward.

It's really a matter of putting positive spiritual energy into our lives instead of negativity It's about looking forward with wisdom and hope, instead of looking back with condemnation and regret. It's about finding ways to make the things that are really important to us happen. The right questions can be very empowering, and they can open new vistas in our lives that we convinced ourselves we would never see.

Remember that the ineffable Spirit is expansive, positive, and full of possibility and opportunity. Changing our questions to be just as positive and expansive can help align us with that energy.

LOOK OUT, WORLD

Often on our daily walks, my partner and I pass a very pregnant, radiant mother and her precious, perhaps precocious three- or four-year-old daughter, both of them decked out in floppy straw hats for sun protection. Sometimes grandma and/or dad are along, both of them looking smitten and somewhat dazed to be walking in the grace and blessings that make up their beautiful family.

The little girl is usually pushing a small baby buggy which never carries a baby. She prefers to walk her unicorn or her McDonald's-kids-meal-sized animals: bears and doggies and dinosaurs. All of them are clearly as loved and cherished as she is.

Last night, we passed them at her house, and our little lady was standing tall on top of a stump in the middle of the front yard. Her mom called over to us and said, "Do you want to know what her new battle cry is?" Of course! Mom lunged into a pose with one foot planted in front and her opposite arm raised at an angle pointing to the sky and cried out, "Look out, world, here I come!" Then she laughed, "If only we could all approach Mondays like that."

If only we could all approach *life* like that! Knowing beyond a shadow of a doubt that we are loved and cared for beyond reason, that we are beautiful inside and out because we see it reflected so strongly in the eyes and actions of those surrounding us. If only we had the courage to live like that little girl, unapologetically ourselves with our hearts open, determined to take the world by storm and make it safe for blue bears and friendly dinos alike.

Somewhere along the line, most of us lose our unabashed confidence in ourselves and the goodness of life. However, the truth that I know to the very core of my being is that the Essence of All That Is loves us and believes in us even more than the most doting, protective, and loving mother or father. We just have a hard time believing it and claiming it and, most of all, receiving it.

Perhaps today we could learn from a child-who-shall-lead-us. Perhaps today we could brandish our invisible swords and banish our self-doubt from our kingdoms and queendoms. Perhaps today we could plant our feet firmly on the ground, saying with a slightly-cocky, knowing smile, "Look out, world, here I come!"

THIS MOMENT IS GOOD

Going a little stir-crazy? Tired of wandering the same rooms of your home? Missing face-to-face conversations and hugs? Wishing you could go do something . . . *anything* . . . but especially something without a mask and involving someone else making food, serving you, and cleaning up? Me, too.

Someone once said that the key to happiness is *loving what you have* instead of wanting what you don't have. Being forced to stay home is a great exercise in learning to love what we have, work on the relationships we've chosen (including our relationship with the Essence of All That Is), and love ourselves.

It's easy some days to get down about our need to isolate. Believe me, I have my moments, too. A few days ago, I was so cranky that I didn't even want to be with myself. I knew it wasn't serving me or anyone around me, but I was kind of stuck. Gratefully, I've never had the sort of disposition to hang onto crabbiness for long. I'm typically a glass half-full kind of person. I tend to remind myself on a regular basis how my life is really good, and I truly don't *need* much of anything.

Humor me and take a moment to look around you and name the things you see that you love . . . a picture on the wall, your favorite chair, a special object given to you by someone special, a picture on the fridge made by your children or grandchildren, a book, a cozy blanket. Be grateful for a moment. Now look at the people you are with (if you are alone, picture a favorite friend or family member), and really *see* them for a moment. Think about their struggles, their fears, their gifts. Think about what has brought them into your life and what you receive (love and/or lessons) from them. Let your heart soften with love for them. Now, gaze at yourself through nonjudgmental eyes of love. See yourself as God sees you – as one who tries hard and is a good person but isn't perfect. Thank your body for all it has done and all it continues to do for you. Send compassion and light to yourself.

Doing this on a consistent basis helps me to remember to love what I have, and then the frustration about what I can't have fades away.

MAKE SOMEONE IMPORTANT

After a major stroke last fall, my dad is now in an assisted living facility close to me. Thankfully, he's the kind of person who can keep himself occupied, even during those early pandemic weeks of isolation without visitors or even a walk down the hall to break up the day.

One Friday, the facility invited family and friends to stage a car parade around the outside of the facility, so my wife Julie, my kids, and I made signs, blew up balloons, decorated my little black Honda Civic with streamers, and circled the complex, waving at the residents and staff watching from their windows. Then we walked to stand below my dad's second-floor window and talked for a while. It was the first time he'd seen us in about six weeks. He hadn't even been able to enjoy my homemade cookies, since we'd been asked not to drop off anything nonessential, but that day I was able to convince a staff member to bring in a bag of cookies and some of his favorite custard for him.

About twenty minutes after we left, he called to say that he'd gotten the goodies, and then his voice got thick with emotion as he said, "Thank you for making me important for a moment." I need an emoji with a tear inserted here, because it choked us all up.

It's easy to become complacent and comfortable in our isolated little worlds, but it doesn't really take much to make someone else feel important for a moment, and it feels so good to do it. Who can you make feel important today?

A FEW SIMPLE WORDS

Never underestimate the power of a few encouraging words. Years ago, on one of the most difficult days of my life, I received an unexpected voice message from a friend that simply said, "I know today is going to be tough, but keep your chin up and smile." It was the last thing I felt like doing. In fact, I was more inclined to dig myself a hole and crawl in. But there was strength and reassurance in that message, perhaps even more so because it came from someone who was battling cancer at the time. He knew what a tough day *really* was. And in the midst of his own struggles, he reached out to *me*. His words became my mantra for that day, and for many days after.

We all have tough days (sometimes even weeks or months) when it feels like the world is caving in. Maybe it isn't always practical to keep our chins up and smile, but I like the way it flies in the face of reason. It defies difficult people and events who try to drag us down. It is hope for better tomorrows and confidence that this too shall pass. And, frankly, sometimes we have to fake it 'til we make it, right? I'm not suggesting we hide our sadness or hurt; it has its place and time. But sometimes we can't get out of the gloomy places until we make the choice to try and emerge. Putting energy into being positive attracts positive energy, and eventually it will be more real than contrived.

This is the balance the spiritual life strives to achieve – being aware of what weighs us down, processing it so that we can release it, and at the same time focusing on our blessings and the positives in life so that we bring light to ourselves and others.

So, keep your chin up and smile! Or if you are already there, then send some encouragement to someone else. A few simple words can go a long way!

YES, LOVE ONE ANOTHER

The larger reality that has become strikingly obvious during this pandemic is that we belong to the community of the world. What happens to people on one side of the globe *does* affect what happens to people on the other side. How people live their lives *does* affect our environment. If we doubted or ignored these things before, we can't any longer (well, it seems some people can, but I don't get that).

So, here's a harder one to wrap our heads around. There were women in Menards last Tuesday who were loudly berating anyone wearing masks for buying into a "government conspiracy." Well, they are part of the community, too. There are also the protesters in many states who are brandishing their weapons and their "freedom" rhetoric, and, in their fear and ignorance, they are cavalier about the well-being of themselves and others. Well, they are part of the community, too. Hmmm . . .

I know there are lots of people like this and that they can make it difficult for us to maintain a sense of benevolence for the human community. I know they push our buttons, annoy us, or just downright piss us off. I get it. Really, Jesus? Love one another? You've got to be absolutely kidding me. Even them?

However, cutting them down and getting angry just doesn't help. The spiritual challenge is to work on understanding, staying positive, erring on the side of compassion, and being a light in the world as often as possible. Each kind, generous, gentle, respectful, loving thing we do or say makes a difference.

We are all connected. We form an intricate and delicate web. This web functions like the safety net beneath the tightrope walker. We must keep it in good repair. Remember the healing power of simply caring. Remind yourself that our hope is built upon a foundation of human kindness. Love until, and even if, it hurts.

TRUSTING THE
CIRCLE OF LIFE

Life is a circle. That seems like an easy thing to remember. Sadly, I'm prone to only seeing to the horizon, forgetting that life goes on after that and opportunities do come around again. Truth be told, the Earth is round, and there are no dragons to be found lurking at the edge. There is life and death and life again, in a multitude of ways. There are beginnings and endings and more beginnings. There is joy and sorrow, and on another day, there will be joy again. I forget.

I forget and get stuck in endings. I'm always sad to finish a good book, because I wish it could go on and on. I love doing puzzles but seriously dislike breaking them apart once we've finally finished. I grieve when something happens and I know that life will never be the same again – because it won't.

Eventually, though, if we continue to engage life, there will be more wonderful things to experience.

You know this as well as I do. We live in the circle of life. We all have had so many endings that we can't even count them, but something always arrives to fill the void. When our abilities change, we find new hobbies and ways to spend our time. When a friend moves away, we slowly find others to spend time with. When we lose loved ones, the world inevitably will start turning again, and we will find new routines, new projects, new ways to find fulfillment.

The spiritual path invites a deeper and deeper trusting of the circle of life. Trust that the Spirit is with us on the journey, working on the beginnings and endings, opening windows and doors, and creating pathways where there were none before. Coming full circle, ironically, always feels like coming home.

GETTING BACK IN THE GAME

It's always hard to maintain one's creative energy for an extended period of time, and the stress of this pandemic certainly doesn't help things any. We finally had a chance to get away for a few days in the hopes of being refreshed, finding new energy, and in my case, discovering fresh ideas for reflections. But this time when we returned, I had a terrible sinking feeling that our wonderful time away had failed, and my river of creativity had all but dried up.

It took me almost a whole day to reengage, and then suddenly I found I had so many ideas running around in my head it was hard to nail one down! What changed, you ask? Here's what I think.

I think transitions are tough, and sometimes we can't actually move on until we've moved on. Do you know what I mean? Reentry from vacation back into work mode, even though I enjoy my vocation, is tough. So, as long as I resisted jumping back in,

I wasn't feeling the new energy I'd found, and I wasn't seeing the new ideas I could explore. I was inadvertently holding myself back.

We face all kinds of different transitions in life, thresholds we have to cross, doors that close in our faces. Too often we stand looking at the closed door and wishing it were still open instead of taking a deep breath, turning around, and applying ourselves to the new day ahead.

We can't really be in two places at once. If I sit and whine about not being on vacation any longer, gazing longingly at the pictures we took of the good times we had, and mope around miserably because I want to be somewhere else, then I've lost whatever beauty and possibility exists in *this* moment.

I know this is harder in certain times more than others. I know grief can keep us standing and looking at that closed door for a long time. And grieving is important for our souls. But, no matter what is behind the door that closed on us, we can carry the love and memories with us while we lean into this sacred, beautiful present day. If you're closing the door on something negative, well, then just leave that there!

Embrace today and all the opportunities for joy, abundance, and adventure that it brings.

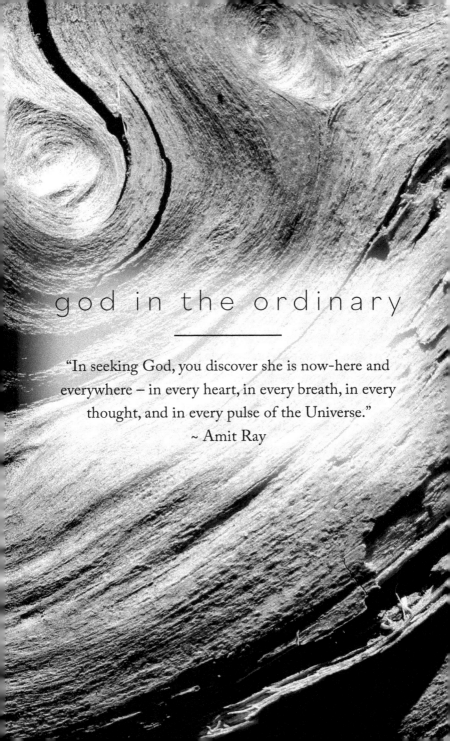

god in the ordinary

"In seeking God, you discover she is now-here and everywhere – in every heart, in every breath, in every thought, and in every pulse of the Universe."
~ Amit Ray

SIGNS

Do you believe in "signs"? I think there is a fear that saying yes makes you sound a little off your rocker, but yes, I do believe in signs. I believe that there is a spiritual thread that runs through all of creation, and the Universe (God, Goddess, Essence, Spirit) can speak to us in a wide variety of ways. Just like dream language is symbolic, so the language of the Spirit is also symbolic.

The interesting thing about signs is how a sign for one person may mean nothing to the next individual. For example, a few months into the pandemic, there was an abundance of owls in my life. First, we were given an owl puzzle (a very difficult, painful puzzle I might add), then we had multiple owl sightings in our backyard and across the street. Plus, I found two owl feathers within a week. Most people might think this was cool, but I recognize the owl as the ancient symbol of the Goddess, wisdom, intuition, and insight. I find great strength in being accompanied by the spirit of this magnificent creature.

The key to receiving the messages of the universe is to open our minds and our hearts and watch for them. Then suddenly, when you need a message of hope, you will find deeper meaning in a butterfly landing suspiciously close to you; or when you need resilience, you'll notice how even the tallest, strongest trees bend in the storms so as not to break; or a line of a song will jump out at you with the advice you need.

We are not alone in this amazing world. Keep your eyes, ears, heart, and mind open, as the Spirit has many creative ways to reach us.

DAILINESS

Joan Chittester, in her book, *Called to Question*, talks about the spiritual challenge of *"dailiness."* She said it is not normally the crises in our lives that get to us, because we know how to summon our reserves of faith and strength and prayer to get through those. It is dealing with normal life that can get stale and boring. It is doing the same mundane tasks, the same job and the same errands, day in and day out, that gets to us.

Stuck in the *Groundhog Day* pandemic world, I appreciated this concept even more. I had the spiritual challenge of writing every day, which helped to keep me grounded and centered; still the days mushed together. I forgot what day of the week it was, and my life outside our small corner called home was defined by how long I could wait to go to the grocery store again.

How we deal with the dailiness, routines, mundane, and ordinary says much about our spiritual state. Do we grit our teeth and keep plodding through the days, waiting for something to entertain us and distract us from those things we wish to ignore? Do we recognize that the Spirit is in everything we plod through, and harness the energy of that Spirit to turn those moments into an appreciation of life itself? Do we seek the extraordinary in the ordinary each and every day?

Once again, the way to enjoy even the most ordinary of days and tasks is awareness, intentionality, and gratitude. Even trying to figure out what to cook *again* becomes sacred when I remember to be grateful that we have food to cook, a beautiful kitchen to cook it in, and a precious family to feed.

How can we change our perspective so this very moment becomes a sacred experience?

GOD IS SINGING

Brother David Steindl-Rast said, "In everything we experience, we can hear God singing, if we listen attentively."

Stop for just a moment. Take a deep breath. Do you hear it? If I pause to intentionally listen for God's singing, I feel the pulse of the universe, or perhaps this is my own heart beating – they are one and the same. Still, it feels like all things pulse, hum, or vibrate with life, energy, and love. I can sink myself into it only to be jarred back by my incessant thoughts and that darn work ethic. Heaven forbid I sit still and simply *be* for a few minutes.

I listen for God's singing in the whisper of the trees or the roar of the wind bringing in a storm. The waves of the ocean carry the Divine voice, as does the gurgling of a stream. But God sings in more than just nature. We can hear the One's song in laughter and love, in concern and caring, in grief and brokenness.

It's harder to identify in the rush of the traffic or the beeping of monitors attached to a loved one, but if we think about it, God's singing – presence, renewing, claiming, comforting, challenging, loving, opening, calming, holding, life-giving – must, by definition, be in all things. We just need to listen.

Where do you hear God's singing today?

INTERRUPTIONS

Over all these years of pastoral ministry, one of the most important things I've discovered is that God is in the interruptions.

When I had a church office to work out of, I always had an open-door policy. Even when I was writing my sermons, I kept my door open, because people who needed me or even just wanted to connect by chit-chatting might have been exactly what I needed at the moment, or I might have been what they needed. I didn't want to literally close the door to the Spirit's ability to work.

That's not to say that I wasn't sometimes irritated by interruptions (I'm not perfect) or exasperated when some seemingly meaningless conversation went on forever (again, not perfect), but I've tried to take a deep breath and remind myself that God is in the interruptions.

What is being interrupted? Why is that so vital?

Why are we so afraid to pause? Why do we believe incessant doing must be the state of our days?

These days, my "interruptions" take the form of my college-aged daughter who is home studying online and occasionally needs something, a dog who wants a walk or to be scratched, and calls from my dad who is in assisted living, among other things. Certainly, this virus has been a huge interruption in our lives, but it has opened new opportunities and possibilities if only we look for them.

The questions to keep asking are, "Where is God in this interruption?" and, "What am I being asked to attend to or release in this moment?"

THAT DARN DISCIPLINE

A number of years ago, I was teaching a class at church and trying to explain how doing something every day – like reading a devotional book, or meditating, or reading scripture, or journaling – just doesn't come naturally for me. I sighed and said, "I'm just not very good at . . . at . . ." and someone chimed in, "discipline."

Yes! That's exactly it! I have such a problem with discipline that I can't even remember the word! So, for those of you who don't actually read these every day and end up catching up at some point (if at all), I completely understand.

I tend to balk at having to do something a certain way every day, though I've always admired those folks who enjoy ritual and discipline. My connections with God tend to be a bit more varied and random; however, they do happen every day.

What has evolved for me is the ability to recognize

the many different ways the Spirit and I connect daily. It may be walking the dog, something I read in a book, the lyrics to a song that pop into my head, the warm feeling of talking with a friend who's known me all my life, playing piano, watching the sunrise, feeling the breeze against my skin . . . It may be almost anything. These sorts of things happen for each of us every day. The "discipline" is the awareness to recognize the Holy in the ordinary.

Today, pay special attention to the Divine in the mundane, in the everyday, and in the chaos. You'll be amazed at where you find the Spirit.

SACRED SPACE

We've forgotten how to live a slower, more reflective, simpler life . . . or perhaps we never knew how in the first place.

There is an addictive quality to watching the news and finding out the latest virus numbers, where the hot spots are, what are the latest vaccine predictions – yada, yada. It's like not being able to take your eyes off the train wreck that's coming. Living this way for a long time sucks the positive, life-affirming, motivating energy right out of us. Yes, we need to stay informed, but we can do that in five-to-ten minutes and then get back to living life!

Perhaps it is simply about remembering our priorities and keeping our focus on what is truly life-giving. How do we remain focused on the Divine and each other? How do we make space for self-reflection, healing, and wholeness? How do we gather up the fragments of our souls and our days?

Here's one idea. I think it would be awesome if we each had spiritual focal points in our homes. Create a small altar or sacred space, one you can see daily and use to re-center. Remind yourself that God is with you, and beauty and blessings exist around you, as does the love which connects us all. You could make it as simple as a candle or one meaningful object which symbolizes your spiritual life. It could include many things: a pretty cloth, pictures of nature or loved ones that you're praying for, pinecones or rocks collected from your yard, sea shells that you picked up at your last visit to the beach (I can't help it, I do this every time we go to a tropical beach) . . . whatever makes you happy. Each time you see it, remember.

I have a sacred space right outside my office door in our loft area and another one in my office. I usually change them seasonally (or whenever I get sick of them), and just the process of assembling something new brings me joy and helps me to focus once more on the One who grounds and sustains me.

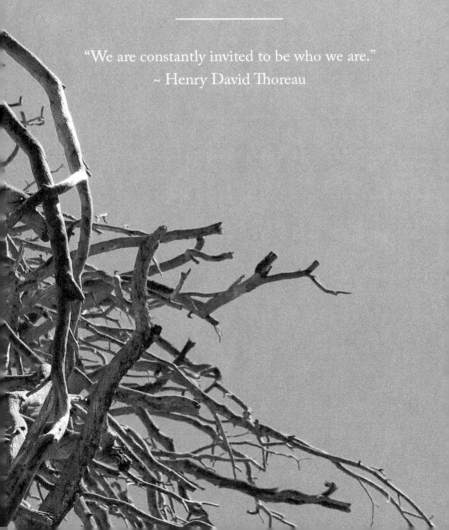

authentic self

"We are constantly invited to be who we are."
~ Henry David Thoreau

KNOW THYSELF

"Know thyself." A form of this phrase can be traced back to ancient Egypt. We could analyze it from a philosophical, psychological, or theological standpoint. However, I'd simply like to be practical.

I'm encouraging you to know thyself so you may come out of these days of isolation with relationships and sanity intact, and perhaps some spiritual growth thrown in for good measure. Know thyself . . . as in, be aware of what you are feeling, why you are feeling it, and how you are behaving because of it. Are you getting bored and irritable? Do you have cabin fever? Do you feel down or lonely? Are you feeling calm and at peace? You get the idea.

Now, if you're calm and peaceful, that's excellent! However, most of those other things have the potential to negatively affect the people you are with, even if you try to hide it. There is an energy to our emotions that can be sensed, especially by people close to us. So, *communicate* how you are feeling! If you don't name and claim it, you risk hurting and/or confusing others through your behaviors or repressed emotions.

Once you are aware of what is going on inside and you own it, then the trick is to determine what you need to do to regain a sense of balance and doing-okay-ness. Do you need space, or do you need to talk? Sometimes I need to journal or do something physical (walking, biking, working outside) or play the piano to get out of a funk. Reaching out to someone else often helps get us out of our own stuff. I like projects, too, like cookie baking or painting a room or doing something creative. What works for you?

Since awareness is an important part of our spirituality, this process is nothing short of a spiritual discipline. Remember, you are free to the degree you are aware. You cannot change that which you cannot even acknowledge. Good luck!

CHUTES AND LADDERS

The spiritual journey is like a game of *Chutes and Ladders*. One day, I feel like I've ascended to new spiritual heights and discovered a deeper level of peace. The next day, I've slipped down the chute into the dark abyss of self-doubt and insecurity. One day, I feel like I am One with all of creation, and I can see the beauty in all things. The next day, all the petty, stupid irritations in life make me cranky, and *I* don't even want to be around myself.

Unlike the real game of *Chutes and Ladders,* this wonderful, maddening spiritual game of ups and downs simply goes on and on. There is no end until our final transition out of these mortal bodies and onto the next adventure.

It's funny, but I know some people feel like since they will never achieve spiritual perfection (after all, they can't *only* land on squares that take them up a ladder), there is no point in trying. However, the goal of the journey, is to keep *moving* toward perfection. There will always be days when we miss the mark or screw up, but overall, if we keep at it, we'll keep inching our way closer to enlightenment (as Buddhists would say). One day, we're helping a little old lady cross the street, and the next day we're cussing a blue streak at the car that just cut us off (okay, I don't do that, but I have my own vices). It happens. Hopefully as time goes on and our awareness grows, there will be more little old ladies (so to speak) and less cussing!

The most important thing is that we keep trying. I believe with all my heart and soul that this spiritual journey, this road to our authentic selves, is worth every hard-fought-for inch.

THE STORY OF OUR SCARS

If you show me yours, I'll show you mine . . . your scars, I mean. Our scars tell stories about us – the times I crashed my bike, the time I weeded the poison ivy patch in my swimsuit, the time I burned myself on the stove, the time I got the chicken pox.

We carry scars on the inside as well. They tell deeper stories about us – the time the kids on the bus called me four-eyes, grabbed my glasses, and threw them around the bus; my dad's critical eye that always found something I could have done better; my mom dying before I could really show her my love and connect with her; the friends who turned their backs on me for reasons I have yet to figure out. And . . . there are more, of course, as there surely are for each of us.

Actually, physical scars aren't as bad as interior wounds that have scabbed over but haven't healed. Those scabs are liable to get scratched or torn off without warning if we don't tend to them. Our spiritual journey to authenticity and wholeness requires us to try and maintain an awareness of what is going on in our hearts, souls, and minds. It requires us to own our wounds before we can heal them. Without healing, we're likely to act out in ways that are unhealthy and hurtful to ourselves or others. Still, we sometimes think it is easier to bury those things deep, and then bury the shovel – but is it?

Dr. Rachel Remen writes, "Whatever we have denied may stop us and dam the creative flow of our lives. Avoiding pain, we may linger in the vicinity of our wounds, sometimes for many years, gathering the courage to experience them. Without reclaiming that which we have denied, we cannot know our wholeness or have our healing."

We need to do the incredibly hard work of healing ourselves, sometimes over and over again, to find peace and live authentically with compassion and light.

PEELING OFF THE LAYERS

Whenever I think of stripping away layers to get to the authentic self, I find myself thinking of *Shrek*. In the animated movie, the ugly, green ogre Shrek is telling his sidekick, Donkey, that ogres have layers. Shortly thereafter, in exasperation, Donkey declares, "Oh, you're so wrapped up in layers, Onion Boy, you're afraid of your own feelings."

I'm a firm believer that underneath all of our layers is a pure, beautiful soul. Look into the eyes of any baby and you'll see the precious, trusting, loving, knowing wisdom and innocence that we're all born with. Without really being aware of what is happening, we slowly cover our core with protective layers, and probably rightly so, to survive in a world which is often less than kind.

But once we hit middle-age-ish, we've come far enough to sense the importance of that pure inner self buried somewhere beneath ego. We catch glimpses when we lose ourselves to a beautiful moment, whether it be a sunset over the water, a piece of music, a kiss, or playing with a child. Suddenly our guard is down, and joy and peace rush in, filling us to the tips of our toes, and we feel whole.

So, here's the challenging part: we can actively *choose* to let go of our layers and experience the fullness of life with which we are one – or not. Sometimes it doesn't feel like a choice, but it is. When the dog rolls in the mud, we can choose to be angry, or we can choose to laugh in oneness with the unabashed joy the dog is experiencing. When someone criticizes us, we can beat ourselves up with it, or we can look at ourselves to see if it is true and then adjust our behavior or let it go, so we do not add another layer. When we feel hurt, we can lash out or withdraw, or we can risk a healing encounter by sticking it out and working through it, even examining our own part in the problem. When we're caught in the rain, we can run for safety and curse the storm gods, or we can dance in it.

Maturity is rooted in making choices.

Making healthy choices is the key to our spiritual growth.

Making good choices is contagious.

Perhaps that is simplifying things too much, but often the simple things are the hardest to do.

A LIFE OF MEANING

Does my life have meaning? I imagine this is a question we've all wrestled with once or twice. It is a profoundly deep question. But I didn't realize it was a flawed question until I read something that Parker Palmer wrote in his book, *On the Brink of Everything*. Basically, he said the question is inherently flawed because it is ego-driven.

It is our ego, not our soul, that wants to make sure we've made an impact on the world – we've succeeded, we've been important, we will be admired and remembered. As soon as this becomes our motivation, we've actually lost the point of living a life of meaning.

I believe to truly live a life of meaning is to be true to one's self and not count the number of people touched, or the number of dollars made, or the number of books sold, or whatever. It makes no difference whether you are a pastor, doctor, teacher, factory worker, or stay-at-home parent. It makes no difference if you live in an apartment or a mansion, if you have one car or five, if you travel to exotic places or go camping. Meaning is an inside job, not an outside acquisition.

As Palmer says, "All I can control are my own intentions, and my willingness to give myself to them: may they always be to serve rather than show off . . . My best offerings come from a deeper, more intuitive place that I can only call my soul."

All that is required to bring real meaning into our lives is to live from the heart, to serve with compassion, and to be true to the Divine Spark within.

ENOUGH ALREADY!

You are enough. That's always been a consistent sermon theme for me. You know they say that pastors really preach to themselves, well, it's true. This is a message I incessantly need to hear.

There are probably a gazillion reasons why we might feel this way: from parents constantly criticizing us, to a coach who humiliated us in front of the team, to being different and being bullied as a result. One woman I met said she had a fairly normal life when she was growing up but always sensed, for most of her life, that she wasn't quite good enough. It sounded to me like this feeling is similar to background music in a store, not blaring, but a steady drone of noise. It took her until midlife to stop dwelling on this negative background music and start focusing on the positive side of her life and herself. It was a beautiful thing to hear but also something many of us have a hard time putting into practice.

Often we beat ourselves up, believing that we've failed ourselves, our families, and our God. As Julia Roberts' character says in *Pretty Woman*, "It's easier to believe the bad stuff." And it doesn't help that so many of our churches have made it perfectly clear we're all sinners (don't even get me started). After those messages have been drilled into our heads or played subliminally as background music for years, it is hard *not* to believe them. This is sad, because I firmly believe it is not what the Holy One wants us to believe.

In case you were wondering, God doesn't dwell on the times we've messed up. God does not keep a naughty and nice list like Santa. God does not keep a running tab of who gets into heaven and who is going to hell (which does not exist, by the way). I believe God is like any good parent, mentor or friend and says, "Okay, so you screwed up. Let's learn and move on." Even more than that, God says, "You are beautiful and unique, with love and skills to share, so please know you are enough!"

We are already enough. We start the class with an A. We begin each day only expected to be present and receive. Enough is all ready to embrace us. Accept the hug.

HOW IS IT WITH YOUR SOUL?

My question of the day is: how is it with your soul? Do you know? Have you checked in with yourself lately? Have you gone down deep inside and waited for some clues, even answers?

Awareness is crucial to the spiritual journey, and it is also vital to surviving well in times of crisis and uncertainty. Being stuck at home during the pandemic, most of us had more time and space to cultivate a deeper communication with our true selves – but my guess is that most of us didn't. As unhappy as the situation is around the world, it is still easier to put our time into reading up on the latest pandemic statistics and protest marches than it is to put time into understanding ourselves and why we do and say the things we do, or using this time to grow more loving, more compassionate, and more connected to the Divine.

I encourage all of us to stop long enough to check

in with our souls and answer ourselves honestly. Are the people you're living with driving you nuts? Is it their fault (which our egos surely say it is), or is it triggering something else in us? Are you feeling safe? Scared? Vulnerable? Are you comfortable with silence, turning off the electronics, and being with yourself? If not, why?

What do you need to do to take care of yourself? Do you need to carve out a little alone time in a house where you are "trapped" with a few other people? Do you need to call a friend and reconnect in a meaningful way with another human being? Do you need to get outside, even if the weather isn't perfect, to feel the energy of nature and let it feed your soul? Do you need to find someone to help you through this time, or through the feelings and emotions that are coming up? Practical help, that is.

Caring for the soul is our spiritual vocation.

SACRED TEARS

Brother Joseph once told of being in the choir at Gethsemane, the monastery he had joined. As they chanted their Latin psalms one day, a baby's cry gently echoed through the vast church. In those days, the monks were kept strictly out of public view, a high screen separating them from the occasional visitor. They knew they would never see the source. Nonetheless, huge smiles spread across the faces of these men even in the midst of their serious and sacred task of praising God, men who had not heard such sound for years, even decades. Brother Joseph recalled looking across the choir – tears were streaming down the face of one of the most stern, ascetic monks in the monastery.

I love this story. It begs me to pause and ask: what do we allow to touch our hearts so deeply that we can be moved to tears? Might the plaintive cry of a child be our hope for the future? Is it the unfolding of the crocus and the strength of the tulip as it pushes up through the hardened soil? Is it the song that pops into your head, unbidden? It is the cacophony of birdsong outside our windows? Is it the tender way our partner holds us, or brushes a crumb from our lips? Is it a picture a child has drawn for us? Is it the day itself, being noticed, being paid honorable attention, being witnessed firsthand?

What will we open ourselves to in such a way that it will connect us intimately to the Spirit that flows through all things and will fill us beyond the brim to overflowing with joy and love? These sorts of tears are not weak but are the most sacred drops of salt water in the universe, because they reveal the truth.

WHO AM I?

Who am I? It must be the quintessential spiritual question. There is a meditation exercise that calls us to keep asking that question over and over again until we have gone deep enough to begin to understand the very core essence of ourselves. Ironically, this pure understanding begins only when we have gone beyond words.

If someone asks us who we are, we tend to very quickly respond with a role we play: I am a mother, a wife, a pastor, a daughter . . . or we respond with characteristics: I am creative, kind, calm (so people tell me), witty, intelligent. But is there more? What is our truest self?

I ask the question today because it feels like we need reminding that we are much more than our physical bodies, the things that we do, and even the things we feel. We are more than people in search of toilet paper and antibacterial wipes. We are more than our fear of germs and getting sick. We are more than our frustration or boredom. We are more than our prayers and beliefs.

We are more. It is my belief that we have always been, and we shall always be, because we are one with the One. We cannot be lost, and we cannot cease to exist. I find comfort, strength, and courage in this. Plus, it allows me to step back and put life in a much broader perspective, and in this I find peace.

SNOW GLOBE SPIRITUALITY

When I was in seminary, I struggled with what it meant to be a pastor. Did I have to act differently? Think differently? Would I find religion and lose my sense of humor? (I've seen it happen.)

It took years, but I finally realized that the spiritual journey doesn't require us to lose ourselves (or our sense of humor). Instead, the journey leads us to find our true selves, and amazingly we find God at the very same time. It would be nice if one soul-searching retreat could enlighten us or if one incredibly inspiring sermon would make everything clear, but the fact is the spiritual journey is a lifelong process of awakening.

Just when I think I'm starting to figure a few things out, just when the snow in my globe is starting to settle and I'm seeing more clearly, someone or something shakes the darn globe again. Sure, it's a little frustrating, but it's exciting, too, because I am challenged to learn more, explore more, experience more.

When my snow globe gets shaken up, I force myself to stop, take a deep breath, and let the tension that I wasn't consciously aware of drain out of my body. Change happens. We will live into the newness one day at a time. Know that we are gently held by a loving God, and trust that things will eventually settle again, and we'll see life with clarity and freshness.

BLOSSOMING

I absolutely love this short poem by Nikos Kazantakis:

I said to the almond tree:
Speak to me of God;
and the almond tree blossomed.

Not only is it a wonderful image of spring bursting forth, but it is also the very essence of how we each can speak of God – by bringing forth the best of our very essence. When we blossom by sharing our authentic selves, by sharing our gifts and skills and talents, and by offering compassion, unconditional love, acceptance, and understanding, it speaks volumes of the Divine Spark that resides in each of us.

It's easy to get caught up in judging the actions (or inaction) of others. It's easy to complain about what we can't do or where we can't go. It's easy to be cynical and sarcastic. It's easy to get caught up in pointing fingers and laying blame. However, none of this really helps the world.

Right now, the world needs each of us to blossom. The world needs us to reach past the layers of fear, anger, grief, and uncertainty to let the budding spark within push through the darkness and burst into the world with pure grace. The world needs us to blossom in kindness and patience, even when it is hard. The world needs us to try to make the best of a bad situation, because how we respond is the only thing under our control. The world needs us to blossom because this, alone, speaks of God. God speaks of hope. Hope is presently our singular and most significant need.

Blossom today . . . the people in your life, and in the world, need you.

courage

"What 'real artists' have is courage. Not enormous gobs of it. Just enough for today . . . Courage, after all, is a matter of heart, and hearts do their work one beat at a time."
~ Julia Cameron, *The Artist's Way*

THE COURAGE TO BE

The gnostic *Gospel of Thomas* says, "If you bring forth what is within you, what you bring forth will save you. If you do not bring forth what is within you, what you do not bring forth will destroy you."

I don't think this was meant to be cryptically difficult. I believe it is straightforward. It is simply saying that each of us has unique gifts and skills to bring to the world, not the least of which is our ability to love. If we live true to ourselves, we will live wholeheartedly and know a depth of living which many people never reach. If we deny, waste, ignore, or bury our spiritual gifts such as compassion and love, and if we refuse to cultivate and use our skills for bringing joy and bettering the world, we will never quite know true fulfillment.

And, yes, we all have skills to share. I know a few people who believe they don't, but even pulling weeds, making a great pot of soup, knitting a scarf, having a meaningful and caring conversation, or playing with a child is a skill to share. Don't look with critical eyes at yourself, but rather with the compassionate eyes of God, who invites you to use what you have in love.

Listening is a great skill, and it is in rare supply. In Elizabeth Gilbert's book, *Big Magic*, she talks about a young, shy college student who shared a story with her one day about a professor named Jack Gilbert (no relation to Elizabeth). One afternoon after Jack's poetry class, he took this young woman aside, complimented her on her work, and asked her what she wanted to do with her life. Hesitantly, she admitted that perhaps she wanted to be a writer.

I have the deepest respect and admiration for Jack's response. He smiled at her with infinite compassion and asked, "Do you have the courage? Do you have the courage to bring forth this work? The treasures that are hidden inside you are hoping you will say yes."

This becomes the question for each of us. Do we have the courage to be who God created us to be? To bring out the best within us? To risk loving? To risk being vulnerable in our sharing of ourselves? And to encourage or challenge others to do the same? I've been told that at the end of life, the things we will regret most are the things we didn't do or chose not to be.

THE UPSIDE OF DOWN

Nelson Mandela once said that he wanted to be judged not by what he accomplished, but by how many times he fell down and got up again. What a statement. He took the emphasis off of all the amazing things he accomplished and reminded us how important it is to keep going, to not give up on our dreams, to stay true to ourselves. Being on a spiritual path doesn't mean we never fall; it just means we understand the falling to be part of the process of growing (even if we'd prefer to skip that part).

Think about how many times you've "fallen" and gotten up again. It starts literally when we are young and learning to walk, and then there are bullies, broken friendships, betrayals, heartbreaks, job losses, failed grades, illnesses, accidents, mistakes, bad investments, rejections, losses, and on and on. Oy! It's amazing that we spend any time standing at all!

I know that sometimes we get terribly bruised and weary from spending so much time on the ground. But I have the greatest respect for those who, time after time, get back up and try again. It always helps me to remember that even a talented author like JK Rowling was rejected twelve times before someone took on her *Harry Potter* stories, John Grisham's first book was rejected by twenty-seven publishers, and Stephen King's first novel was rejected thirty times. Frankly, I'm not sure I could have kept going, but I am in awe of their tenacity and resilience.

Sometimes to keep going, it helps to narrow our focus to the next step. Thinking about the five hundred or so sermons I have to preach before I retire makes my head spin . . . but the next one, I can handle the next one.

So, if you've recently been spending some time on the ground, take a deep breath and concentrate on just one thing, one day, one step. And be proud of yourself. It's life, and you're living it!

CHOOSE LIFE

In 2001, I met Mike at a "Preach-in" in Naramata, Canada, where I spent six days with fourteen other pastors of seven denominations from all over the U.S. and Canada. Together we danced with the Scriptures and worked to create part of a preaching resource for pastors.

Mike was our leader who began our week by sharing his amazing story. When Mike was born, he was diagnosed with Cystic Fibrosis and wasn't expected to live more than a few years. Those few years came and went, and he was given another few years, and then another few and another few. As a result, he lived with the constant thought that he would die sooner than later. His health deteriorated to the point of needing a double lung transplant. It was either that or death.

Oddly enough, this was a hard decision for Mike. He had lived with the idea of dying for so long that he was afraid to live. What would it mean to live? What would he do with his life? What if he came out of the surgery an invalid? Finally, he decided that he didn't want to be defined by his fear of living. At the age of thirty, he had a successful lung transplant.

I constantly hope and pray that all of you are being cautious and safe during this uncertain time. However, I also hope that none of us will become so paralyzed and anxious by the thought of this virus that we are afraid to live. Perhaps our living is defined a bit differently these days, but we are still alive. There is no point to deadening the day, as every day has its challenges, and we have managed to get through thousands of them already. Instead, may we find safe ways to enjoy relationships, nature, beauty, friendships, fun, and spirituality. Choose life!

RESILIENCE

Resilience: it's how we get through the trying, difficult, often painful times in life. We will all need an extra dose of resiliency to make it through not only this time of Safer at Home, but also the economic downturn, the fear of another wave of the virus, the paranoia of being near other people, the gaping divides between people, and the sadness of all we've missed or will miss. Many people are also grieving the loss of loved ones. I'm afraid the ramifications of this pandemic are seemingly endless.

Brené Brown, research professor at the University of Houston, found that one of the key factors in people's resiliency was spirituality. Not religion or a set of beliefs, but spirituality. In her book, *The Gifts of Imperfection*, she writes, "Without exception, spirituality – the belief in connection, a power greater than self, and interconnections grounded in love and compassion – emerged as a component of resilience."

I have a friend who tells me that holding the soft, tiny hand of his grandson is an amazing source of resilience for him and brings him a deep sense of balance. I believe it is in those simple moments of touch and human connection that we also touch the eternal essence that exists through lifetime after lifetime.

There is a mystical knowing of the Divine inherent to each spiritual journey. It is a deep, intuitive sense that there is more to life and more to our very selves than is apparent to the eye. Along with this knowing comes the strength, hope, and courage to keep putting one foot in front of the other. We are resilient, we will bounce back, we will go on – it just may take some time.

BELIEVE IN YOURSELF

In an article in *Psychology Today* entitled "The Art of Resilience," Hara Estroff Marano writes that in addition to being spiritual, a belief in oneself is essential to resilience.

Coincidentally, I have a cute little journal that was given to me a few years ago that sits on my desk, and its cover says, "BELIEVE IN YOURSELF." It's empty. I haven't known what to write in it. It seemed like it should be something profound and pertinent to the cover. It's not that I don't believe in myself, but it just seems egotistical to talk about it. I suppose that sounds ridiculous, and I'm probably making too much out of it, but there you have it.

Anyway, it's true that bouncing back when things get tough goes a whole lot better when you believe you have the capacity to do just that. Part of believing in ourselves stems from experience. We've been there, done that. It may not have been easy or fun, but we're still going. So, certainly we can make it through one more thing.

Marano reminds us, "Resilient people don't walk between the raindrops; they have scars to show for their experience. They struggle – but keep functioning anyway. Resilience is not the ability to escape unharmed."

To clarify a bit, believing in oneself *does not* mean we have to go it alone! It means that, in addition to trusting our own inner strength, abilities, and track record, we believe we have the resources available to tap into if we need them. We have friends we can call, family who will support us, neighbors who are standing by, and we're not afraid, or embarrassed, or too stubborn to ask for help.

For today, consider finishing these three phrases with your strengths and resources:

I have . . .
I am . . .
I can . . .

The first three pages of my little journal are now filled in with the answers to these, and it feels good.

Let me close with one of my favorite quotes from *Winnie the Pooh*, "Always remember: you are braver than you believe, and stronger than you seem, and smarter than you think."

DRINKING TO THE DREGS

As the story goes, just before Jesus took his last breath on the cross, he proclaimed that he was thirsty, so someone soaked a sponge with sour wine and touched it to his mouth. Well, sour wine isn't exactly dregs, but (work with me here) it still reminds me of our saying about "drinking life to the dregs." In other words, living life to its fullest, including all of the highest highs and lowest lows. If anyone had dregs in their cup, it was Jesus.

Have you ever slammed back that last slug of coffee or wine only to find yourself with an unexpected mouthful of gritty stuff? Just thinking about it sort of makes me want to gag. Seems like it would be safer putting the glass down before getting anywhere close to the bottom just to avoid the possibility.

There was only one point we know of when Jesus wanted to give up and put the cup down. In the Garden of Gethsemane, we're told he prayed, "Let this cup pass me by," but there was no going back. He'd marched on Jerusalem (sort of reminds me of marching on Washington), pissed off the Roman and Jewish authorities, and the powers that be were already tipped off to his location and on their way to arrest him. However, at any earlier point he could have refused to drink. He could have put the proverbial cup down and walked away. He could have quietly stopped preaching and teaching and lived out the rest of his life as a carpenter. But then ... he wouldn't have been true to himself or to God.

Even during the most difficult days, may we each have the courage to live true to the light within each of us, acting with great compassion, striving to be as positive as possible, and showing kindness, love, caring, and hope. We will need all of our courage and strength to take all that life sends us when we live our truth, stand up for what we believe in, love unconditionally, and drink to the dregs.

transformation

———

"When the time is right, the cocooned soul
begins to emerge. Waiting turns golden. Newness
unfurls. It's a time of pure, unmitigated wonder.
Yet as we enter the passage of emergence, we
need to remember that new life comes slowly,
awkwardly, on wobbly wings."
~ Sue Monk Kidd, *When the Heart Waits*

SPIRITUAL TRANSFORMATION

So, here's an interesting thought, see if you can follow me ... If dying is our final stage of growth, *and* we experience small deaths throughout our lifetime (for example: the death of our childhood, innocence, singleness, friendships, abilities, and so forth), *and* we could consider this time of isolation a certain type of death (of the way things were, of things canceled, etc.), *then* this could be an intense time of personal growth.

Growing involves stripping away layers of ourselves to become more authentic. This may not be easy for some of us. Without the blanket of busyness that we used to wrap up in, we're forced to spend more time with ourselves, our thoughts and feelings, and our shadow sides. Our shadow sides are the darker parts of ourselves we don't like to look at, but which follow us around nonetheless. It is emotions like anger, guilt, lack of self-esteem, and shame, that we choose not to address; consequently, they subconsciously affect what we do and say, often to our detriment.

Elisabeth Kubler-Ross wrote, "Transformation of our lives for the good begins as we commit ourselves to the experiencing of our own identity, a commitment to answering the question: Who am I? Now. Here. This is the first level of religious commitment."

If we're truly interested in spiritual transformation, we won't shy away from the tough stuff at this time. Instead, we'll tackle the tough questions that arise. Why am I grumpy today? Why are my buttons getting pushed so easily? Why am I feeling so down? Who is God to me during all this? Who am I without all of the *things* I used to do? What is the meaning of life? What is my purpose? What is really important?

Think about it. Talk about it. Write about it. The exploration of these questions and the growth it enables to happen are essential to becoming whole and wise.

SAME OLD, SAME OLD

For a long time, when I'd talk to people on the phone during this pandemic and they'd ask how I was doing, my answers were pretty boring. "Fine." "Not much new here." "Same old, same old."

Then I discovered that it was still possible to do new things, and those new things made me feel more alive, more hopeful, and happier. As an added bonus, my dad's neurologist told him the best thing for his brain (aside from exercise) was trying new things and doing things that challenge him. It was clearly time to branch out.

The first thing I did was ask a friend to teach me (online) how to paint with watercolors. It was so exciting just to purchase the supplies. Even preparing for this new adventure was enlivening. Suddenly my evening hours were being used productively and creatively, and my soul perked up.

The second thing my partner and I did was

purchase inflatable kayaks. It sounds sort of cheesy and flimsy, but they were a good quality, and we were thrilled to get out of the house and explore lakes and rivers that we'd never seen. Being out in the beauty of nature, with only the sound of our paddles dipping into the water to keep us company, was rejuvenating.

We can't simply hold our breath and put life on hold until we can do all the things we used to. It's time to put energy into that which we *can* do. Learn to bake bread, take an online course, try writing poetry, plant some vegetables, take up bird-watching, learn to meditate, make a new recipe, do whatever interests you.

This is also a great time to reach out to others. Make a call to someone you know who lives alone. Write a "Thinking of You" card. Send a gift just for fun. Even an email or two can perk someone up and make your soul smile at the same time.

Challenge yourself to find something new to try this week; it's good for your soul, and it's good for your brain, too!

THE GIFT OF AN ITCH

Years ago, I was leading a women's retreat, at the end of which I asked for feedback and constructive criticism so as to make future retreats better. There was one comment that made me sigh and inwardly roll my eyes. *I want a bigger chair.*

Really? A whole weekend of deep conversation, meditation, art, time away at a great retreat center, amazing women, and all I get is, "I want a bigger chair"? Which, of course, I have no control of anyway.

Does everything in life come down to how comfortable we are? We don't try new things because we'd be uncomfortable. We don't want to have the important but difficult conversations because we'd be uncomfortable. We don't want to do something alone, even though it is really important to our soul, because we'd be uncomfortable. We don't want to wear a mask, even though it is essential for our health and others', because we'd be uncomfortable.

We don't want to face our own baggage, dark sides, judgmentalism, and prejudices because it would be uncomfortable. Honestly, I could go on and on . . . you know I could. We all could.

But what kind of life are you living if you're comfortable all the time? I'm going out on a limb here, but I think it would be a very boring, mundane, lifeless life. It would be like going to an ice cream parlor where they only have vanilla and chocolate.

Being uncomfortable is not always great (like in the dentist's chair), but in a physically pain-free way, being uncomfortable can be exciting because it means we're learning and growing. So, let go of some of the whininess about being uncomfortable, suck it up, and engage the amazing life you were given!

KEEP GOING

In May of 1940, when the British seemed all but finished against the vicious and victorious Nazis, Winston Churchill took over the job as Prime Minister. Within two weeks, the United Kingdom was the only country in Europe left standing. Churchill didn't pull any punches; he didn't lie or hide behind a smoke screen of clichés and false optimism. Instead, with complete honesty, he told the British people that all he had to offer was his own "blood, toil, tears and sweat," and rallied them with pride and determination to "never, never, never give up." Perhaps my favorite quote of his is, "If you're going through hell, keep going."

Between the virus and the latest (because this is not new) racial injustices and tension, it sort of feels like we've entered a new version of hell where life as we knew it has all but disappeared, and we're not quite sure when or how we're going to level out to a new normal. Still, it seems to me that the key is to keep moving forward, one step at a time, just like society has every time life has been thrown into chaos.

Just in the last hundred years or so, the U.S. has had its "normal" disrupted multiple times by World War I, the Spanish Flu, the Great Depression, World War II, polio, the Civil Rights Movement, the Equal Rights Movement, the Vietnam War, the Gulf War, AIDS, and 9/11 (and I probably missed a few since history was never my best subject). People went through hell to greater and lesser degrees with all of those, but as a whole we kept going. With resilience, strength, and determination – and by helping one another – life continued, stabilized, and eventually flourished once again. Things were different after each event, certainly, but that doesn't mean life was bad.

No "normal" ever lasts forever. Change is truly the only constant; this is the promise of a Higher Power who makes all things new. Sure, we prefer slow change where we can adjust almost imperceptibly, but it just doesn't always work that way. One day, this too will simply be another marker on a historical timeline. We'll see this through. Just hang on, and for heaven's sake, keep going.

THE GREAT PROMISE OF A BIG MESS

Last summer, I found an idea on Pinterest that was the perfect addition to our guest bedroom – a bookcase made from an old six-panel door. It took me a bit to track down a door, but I finally picked one up for $30.

The door was in pretty rough shape, but that was going to be part of the character. My partner didn't like my concept of character much and tried to fill in some of the larger gashes with wood filler when I wasn't looking! In any case, with a great deal of help from my wonderful neighbor, we got the shelves finished. It has taken me much sanding and many coats of stain, paint, and poly to finally get it to the point of putting books on it, but I'm thrilled with the results.

Now, not only do I have a literal doorway into a land of great stories, but there is also something very satisfying about taking something old, honoring its character and value, and transforming it into something useful again. I've also learned that the process of transformation takes longer than expected (or longer than I'd like) and involves quite a bit of trial and error. Plus, sometimes ideas don't work, and it's always a messy process.

As the queen of metaphors, I'm completely comfortable turning this into an allegory of the spiritual journey. Our personal spiritual transformation requires time and effort; it doesn't just happen overnight. We have to keep working on it, trying new spiritual practices, reading new books, talking to people, and actively engaging the path to get anywhere. Some things will resonate with us, and some things won't. Such is life. And occasionally (though hopefully not often), we'll find we have to backtrack and try a new path. Finally, it strikes me that the whole process can indeed be quite messy and challenging. We're apt to encounter conflicting ideas and experience tension between what we thought we knew and what we're discovering. Staying with the process, however, can be very satisfying, eventually leading us to a new level of insight and awareness.

While I may have finished my bookcase, that doesn't mean I'm done! This is also true of my spirituality. However, I am committed to keep engaging the process which makes life an exciting, ongoing adventure of growth and transformation.

THE BROKEN MUG

I broke my favorite mug on Sunday. One second, I was putting it in the cupboard, and the next it slipped and fell onto the granite countertop, and the handle broke off. I was crushed, which sounds silly even to me. It's a mug, for Pete's sake. But it was given to me by a wonderful parishioner who passed away a few years ago. I remember her, her kindness, and her thoughtfulness every morning when I have my cup of tea. Plus, it was the perfect size and shape in my hands. Gluing it didn't work, either. It wouldn't even go back together right. And even if it had, I'd never really trust that it wouldn't break in my hand.

Paying close attention to this odd grief over a mug, I came to realize that other losses – past, present and future – were creeping into the mix. Who knew they were so close to the surface?

The lessons I've been reflecting on from this experience are numerous. Life is fragile. Sometimes things are too broken to fix. We're vulnerable in those places where we've been broken. We need to work through grief over and over again. Tears are cleansing. Hugs are helpful. And tragedy is great fodder for songs, poems, and spiritual reflections.

I'm also reminded of the Buddhist adage: attachment causes suffering. Even those tiny ties to things which others might find insignificant can cause anguish when taken away.

It's amazing what one can learn from an ordinary broken mug.

In the end, life goes on . . . I reluctantly picked another mug and had my tea. In the spirit of healing, perhaps today would be a good day to buy a mug and some tea for someone else.

THE ANSWER IS BLOWING IN
THE WIND

Of all the images of God, the Spirit (manifested scripturally as fire and wind) is one of my favorites. She's the one who blows through closed doors and sets our heads and hearts on fire. She is anything but quiet, demure, and unassuming. Nope, the Spirit kicks down the doors, rattles the windows, and knocks down walls. If we allow her into our spiritual communities and our lives, we will find ourselves challenged, sent forth, and called out of our comfort zones. So, if you like your comfort zone, if you like a quiet, peaceful, traditional, spiritual practice . . . you will *not* be happy to see the Spirit blow in.

To follow the Spirit of God, one needs to be ready to move beyond the settled, cozy religious club of people who appear to be clones. The church needs to open itself wide, stretch, reach out, and soar. It cannot be content to march in place, as faith is never all talk or stagnation, but is a walk guided by the Spirit of Wholeness. The Breath of Life wants us to grow spiritually, not on our own designs, but on the basis of living God's constant call to love.

I'm pretty sure that God does *not* look at this world and say, "Oh, it's okay, you don't have to change anymore, the world is perfect just as it is." God loves us no matter what, but because we are beloved, the Spirit is continually pushing us to change and grow into fully becoming what we were created to be. Until every creature continually dwells in love, we have not arrived at what we can become. Until all people are equal, until all people are fed, until all people are safe, until all people have health care, until all people have opportunities for education, until all people live in peace, the Spirit will not be done with us.

The next windy day or night, go outside and sit in it – the wind, that is. It is amazingly powerful, present, and, like the Spirit, working all the time to shift the terrain even a little bit. I believe the Spirit is ready to blow in each of our lives if we are ready for new beginnings, new hope, new relationships, new adventures . . . if we are ready for *change*! If you're not ready for change, don't invite the Spirit in . . . Don't even whisper, "Come, Holy Spirit, come."

THAT DARN DOG

One balmy, lime green spring day, I was getting ready to cook some Italian chicken sausage on the grill for lunch. I set the plate of sausage down for a minute to go in search of the lighter. I swear I wasn't gone for more than a minute, but when I returned, two of the four sausages were gone, and one was on the ground. That darn dog!

Well, the moral of the story is this. One, don't turn your back on a dog when food is around. And, two, everything can change in the blink of an eye. We all know this, even if we don't always like it. It strikes me that many of my negative feelings are the result of changes I didn't like. Regret, anger, shame, guilt, fear, jealousy, sadness, and others often occur when I'm not handling change well – if at all.

Imagine, for a moment, if life could stop dead in its tracks and *didn't* change. Can you name a time you would choose to stay put without change? Forever?

I'm afraid that even the best moments, the ones we think we'd like to dwell in for a long, long time, would eventually grow stale and we'd get restless. Hmmm . . . maybe life without change isn't so appealing after all. Besides, how could I freeze time at only one point in life, with only certain people, with no opportunity to learn, grow, mature, or gain wisdom? And I'd be insisting that everyone else around me stop changing as well.

I also recognize that with each "negative" change in my life, there have always been positive pieces to it (eventually), like new friends, new opportunities, or new and important things I've learned about life or myself. Could I really choose to forgo some of those things? I'm tempted to say yes about some things, but we are who we are because of what we've been through.

The spiritual journey recognizes that change *is* the path. Dogs steal our sausages, life happens, and there is no way around that. The only option becomes how well we accept and handle change, small and large.

In case you were curious, the dog still lives. We thawed another sausage and went on. She still had the audacity to beg for more, though.

REMEMBERING THIS
PARTICULAR MOMENT

Early in the pandemic, a friend told me that she sent her grandchildren postcards and asked them, "How will you remember this time in your life?" I think that is a great question.

How we remember this time is, at least in part, up to us. Will we remember this as the time of the great toilet paper run of 2020? Will we remember this as a time of being glued to the television and online news, watching obsessively as the death toll climbed and nations around the world struggled to bring the virus under control? Will we remember this as a time of loneliness and isolation, feeling the great loss of human contact? Will we remember this as the time when we missed out on weddings and birthdays, singing in the Easter choir, and canceled concerts and sporting events? Will we remember this time by the crash of the stock market and the loss of jobs? It may be inevitable that we remember this time by the people we lose. I'm sure all of these things will be part of our collective memory, but how we remember this time doesn't have to stop there.

I've watched the amazing creativity and resilience of people as they have come to accept this situation and found new ways to connect and to respond in helpful, compassionate ways. Perhaps we'll remember this as a time when families grew closer because parents worked at home and kids couldn't go hang with their friends. Perhaps we'll remember this as the time we all learned how to use online ways to see our loved ones, had virtual happy hours with our friends, and shared birthdays, wedding showers, and more on our computers.

Perhaps we'll remember how neighbors reached out (without touching) by decorating doors and windows with construction-paper hearts, sidewalk chalk messages, and teddy bears sitting in windows for kids to count.

Perhaps we'll remember how much we got done! All the rooms we painted, the closets we cleaned, the fantastic looking yards, the puzzles we did together, the books we read, the new recipes we tried.

Perhaps we'll remember how companies stepped up (or didn't) to take care of their employees and customers.

Hopefully, we'll remember this as a time of solidarity, when people set aside their differences and remembered our shared humanity by being gentler, kinder, more understanding, and compassionate. Whether in the midst of a world crisis or not, it behooves us to contemplate what memories we want to create in our lives. How is it we wish to say we lived?

spirituality
takes practice,
practice, practice

"For most of us, the reality is that spiritual growth is like learning to walk. We stand up, fall, stand up, fall, take a step, fall, take a cuple of steps, fall, walk a little better, wobble a bit, fall, run, walk, and finally, eventually fly."

~ Geri Larkin, *Stumbling Toward Enlightenment*

MERCY MAGNIFIED

A dear friend reminded me that healing our inner wounds often begins with forgiveness – of ourselves as well as others. But here's the deal: forgiveness has very little to do with anyone else. It doesn't rely on them asking for forgiveness, nor on you saying you're sorry. The power of forgiveness is found in the brief moments when you've *truly* touched forgiveness and discovered peace within yourself, and you recognize you will not give anyone or anything the power to disrupt it.

Forgiveness does *not* necessarily mean forgetting what happened. After all, we want (or need) to learn from our mistakes as well as from the wrongs others have done to us. We also don't want to set ourselves up to get hurt again. However, healing requires letting go of the anger towards ourselves and others so that it stops eating away at us. Such anger can devour our soul and our days.

Truthfully, forgiveness is one of the messiest things I can think of. We don't want to feel awful, stuck in hurt, pain, and/or anger. However, we don't want to let someone else, much less ourselves, off the hook too easily. I think part of us *wants* to see punishment inflicted, as sad as that sounds. We're typically even worse on ourselves than on others. *I should have known better. I don't deserve to be forgiven. I can't let it go or it looks like I don't care* – and on and on.

I know some days I'm pretty good at forgiveness. But then I can jump right back into anger and hurt, or guilt and shame, when the right button gets pushed. My continual task is to keep working on letting go and reclaiming my inherent sacred worth, tarnished though my halo may be.

I loved microscopes as a kid. Putting bits of creation on glass slides and getting to see a whole new world through the lens was fascinating. Forgiveness is much the same as a microscope. It will magnify the raw goodness you forgot was within you or never even knew existed.

THE CURSE OF COMPARING

I took a Zoom watercolor class during the Safer at Home order. Every other week we would get started on a painting together and then finish on our own. As much as I tried to make my paintings look like the teacher's, I always failed miserably.

Our teacher has such an easy touch about her that makes all of her paintings look simple, yet beautiful – soft, yet distinct. If I were an art critic, I'm sure I could say this much better. The other student in the class has more experience with acrylics and oils and often bemoans the fact that her paintings are too dark. Personally, I view her paintings as bold and lifelike, more detailed and intense. I look at both of their finished paintings while I'm trying to finish mine, and I don't know who I want to be! This makes me a bit pouty, frustrated by my inability to be as good as either of them.

I find it fascinating that three of us can work off

of the same photo and yet our paintings look very different. I don't necessarily mean this in terms of better and worse, but rather in terms of color and look and emphasis. It finally hit me how we all have our own style! Well, maybe I'm still trying to figure mine out, but you get what I'm saying. We're different people; we have different perspectives, different ways of doing things, different likes and dislikes – and it's all good.

I'm afraid it's all too easy to fall into the trap of comparing ourselves to others. I know, intellectually, that comparing myself to others (where I am never as good) is simply a recipe for unhappiness. It will immediately take the joy out of learning watercolors if I constantly trade the fun of learning for the misery of judging myself as not good enough. Who cares? I'm not going to be another Georgia O'Keefe, but so what? The spiritual path is about living fully in the present moment. If I can simply learn to enjoy the process of creating, then I've gifted myself with something precious.

Yes, comparing can be inspiring – even creative – but boy, it can also be one big curse. Whenever we begin comparing our artistic abilities, our writing skills, our looks, our talents, our accomplishments, our yards, or how good of parents we are, we immediately do ourselves a disservice. It's hard to ever win if we're comparing. And if we "win," it's only because we've put someone else down as "not good enough."

An article from the *Farnam Street* blog entitled, "The Danger of Comparing Yourself to Others," suggests that the only scorecard we need to keep is an inner one where we strive to be the best person we can be. The author asks, "Are you better than you were when you woke up? If not, you've wasted a day. It's less about others and more about how you improve relative to who you were. When you stop comparing between people and focus internally, you start being better at what really matters: being you. It's simple but not easy."

THE POISON TREE

There seems to be no shortage of challenges and difficulties in life, and only some of them have to do with the pandemic. The question becomes: how do we deal with them? How do we respond to obstacles, disappointments, frustrations, and crushed expectations?

Buddhist teacher and author, Jack Kornfield, in his book *A Path with Heart*, uses the story of the poison tree to describe three stages of spiritual maturity which guide how we deal with difficult situations. The story goes like this . . .

Once upon a time, there was a poison tree. Upon discovering the tree, some people immediately wanted to cut it down because they saw it as dangerous and a threat to everyone. Another group of people responded instead with compassion for the tree. They suggested putting a fence up around the tree to keep people safe, while still allowing the tree to survive.

And a third group of people looked at the poison tree and thought, "A poison tree, just what I need!" That group picked the fruit, analyzed its properties, and used it as a great medicine to help heal the sick.

The first group of people represents our knee-jerk reaction to things we perceive as negative – get rid of it! Preferably as quickly as possible! Or, at the very least, avoid it at all costs. I totally understand this. Just when life seems to be going along pretty well, inevitably something happens to destroy my nice, calm, sunshiny ride. It's hard to embrace these things at the outset and much easier to whine, rage, ignore, or shut out whatever it is.

The second group of people represents those times when we are able to take a step back and open up to all of life with compassion and a desire to understand. It does not allow judgment and fear to take hold. I practice this one a lot, which is not to say that I don't need more practice. Deep breath . . . we are all one.

The third group represents the best in ourselves, our highest spiritual evolution, where we are able to see the situation in a way most people cannot and find value even in the most difficult of times. Ugh. This one is really tough in the moment. It's much easier when you're looking back from time and distance to see the gifts brought by something challenging.

It seems apparent to me that at any given time, we don't live in only one of these stages. However, I share this with you because it offers an interesting way to reflect on ourselves and our lives. It's especially interesting to apply it to these crazy times when we'd just like the virus to go away. Since that isn't going to happen, can we get to a place where we see what the pandemic might be teaching us about life, about ourselves and our relationships, about priorities, about freedom, and about the Divine? Let's find out what gifts and opportunities our "poison trees" have for us.

KEEP THE FAITH

Years ago, on a mission trip to Appalachia, our six-person crew was assigned to Miss Judy's house. As happens in Appalachia where the houses are built into the sides of the mountains, when it rains, the water runs down the slope and under the house, and eventually rots everything out.

The previous crew had dug a small drainage ditch across the back of the house to catch the water and funnel it around the side of the house and down the hill. Unfortunately, they had filled it with gravel that wasn't heavy enough, so it washed down the hill with the next good rain. One of our jobs, in addition to scraping and painting the house and replacing the rotten, termite-infested back wall, was to put heavier stones in that ditch.

We waited and waited for that stone to be delivered. Finally, it was our last day, and it still hadn't arrived by lunchtime. The family wasn't around, so we took ourselves out for lunch at the nearby Pizza Hut. When we returned, there it was! Four tons of heavy gravel and good-sized rocks (like football-sized) and just a few hours to move it before we were done for the week and headed home.

First things first . . . gloves. Where the heck were my gloves? My old, worn, dirty, beloved gloves that had been on every mission trip with me. I looked all over and then remembered that earlier I had seen them lying in the middle of the driveway with a bunch of other things. Yep, you guessed it, my gloves were under that four-ton pile of rock!

We worked like crazy for the next four hours, putting two people on a wheelbarrow to push the stone up the hill and behind the house. There were a few moments of hysteria, born of sheer exhaustion, but by five p.m. we were scraping away the last of the stones, and there, flat as a pancake on a hot southern griddle, were my gloves! In a very rare show of religiosity, I flopped to my knees and said a silent prayer of gratitude.

Before we left, we found a large flat rock, grabbed a black marker, and left the family a note: *Keep the Faith*. Signed by each of us.

That's still the message today: *keep the faith*. Faith that together we will get through the tough times. Faith that even when things seem impossible, there is a way. Faith that better days are ahead. Faith that the Divine is with us, even when it doesn't feel like it. Faith that there are still plenty of good people out there. Faith that love will eventually conquer hate. Faith that when you put your mind to something and you're working with a great group of people, amazing things can be accomplished.

THE COMFORT OF RITUALS

Ritual. It's sort of a stuffy word relegated to the grand, vaulted ceilings of churches. According to Google, a ritual is "a religious or solemn ceremony consisting of a series of actions performed according to a prescribed order." But ritual is much more than that, and I wonder if some of our angst and frustration with this pandemic time has to do with the disruption of our rituals.

For those of you brought up in highly liturgical churches (Catholic and Episcopal especially), you may understand better how doing the same thing over and over again can bring a sense of grounding and comfort as you wrap yourself once again in the familiar sounds, smells, tastes, and actions of worship. I know a number of people who just can't leave those religious rituals even though they don't believe much of what those churches espouse any longer.

In my small spiritual community, our rituals

are a little more informal. Greeting one another at the beginning of worship, joining our voices in song, sharing our joys and concerns, watching in fascination as "Pastor Kaye" wrangles with the children at Kids' Time, gathering our gifts in offering, and coffee hour are (or were) all weekly rituals. The fact that so many people choose to sit in roughly (or exactly) the same spot each week is a ritual, too.

Just thinking about these things stirs up feelings of longing. But I know we have other personal rituals that may have been upended. Maybe coffee with special friends has been temporarily halted (and Zoom just isn't the same), or the art fair you go to every summer isn't happening, or you have more people at home and less private time to just "be," or your annual trip was canceled, or your theater dates have been postponed, or you can't sit in your regular booth for the Friday night fish fry. I bet you can add to the list.

These rituals, as ordinary as they seem, take on a sacred quality when they serve to comfort, ground, and center us. Without the fireworks, without the yearly family picnic, without being able to attend funerals and weddings, without the usual big birthday parties, and without church, it sort of feels like the rug has been pulled out from under us.

What rituals have you missed most? Have you developed any new rituals during this time? Do you have rituals that help connect you to the Divine? If not, is there something you could do that would help put that rug back under you? Or at least something that could be a temporary crutch until we're all back on our feet?

I know things are going to be different for a while, but I do believe that someday we will be able to return to most of the rituals – small and large, communal and personal – that brought us so much joy.

A SACRED PAUSE

Robert Fulghum, in his book *From Beginning to End: The Rituals of Our Lives* writes, "Rituals do not always involve words, occasions, officials, or an audience. Rituals are often silent, solitary, and self-contained. The most powerful rites of passage are reflective – when you look back on your life again and again, paying attention to the rivers you have crossed and the gates you have opened and walked on through, the thresholds you have passed over."

Do you ever do this? Sit and mull over the past . . . the path you've taken . . . the choices you've made . . . the synchronicities that brought seemingly impossible things together . . . the times you'd like to edit out . . . the perfect moments or days you wish you could revisit . . . I do, but I never really thought about it as a ritual before.

In his book, Fulghum talks about occasionally taking a lawn chair to the grave site that he purchased for himself and sitting for a while to pay his respects to his final resting place. He claims it always serves to bring perspective to bouts of anger, frustration, irritation, and life itself.

Perhaps this is what looking our lives over can do for us – it's a sacred pause to remember what we've been through, the tough times we've survived, how we've learned and grown in wisdom, and how at the end of the day, it's better to be above ground than below ground. Life is worthy of review, and taking the time to do so – a sacred pause – is just plain smart.

No matter how much time we have left, or how little, we can still give all of ourselves to making each precious moment count.

A SCARY PRAYER

Here's a scary prayer from the works of Saint Teresa of Avila:

I am Yours and born for You.
What do You want of me?

You've heard the saying, "Don't ask the question if you don't want to hear the answer." It seems like this is one of those questions most of us probably don't ask because, really, do we want to know what God wants of us?

That sounds a little scary to me. I'm much more comfortable praying for healing for Josie, or strength for Arthur, or help for my own personal struggles. I'm not sure I want to know that God is asking more patience of me, or how I need to forgive someone who hurt me deeply, or I need to suck it up and apologize, or step up and volunteer at the hot meal program, or be nicer and more understanding of those who vote differently than I do – or whatever.

I'd venture to say that most of our prayers, while not necessarily selfish, are focused on ourselves, our gratitude, our needs, and the needs of those around us. And there is nothing wrong with these prayers; I'd just suggest that we spend a lot of time trying to get the Divine aligned with us, while this prayer of Teresa's seeks to align *us* with the Divine.

What would happen if the next time we got angry, we asked, "God, what do you want of me?" What would happen if the next time we were faced with a difficult decision or situation, we prayed, "Holy One, what do you want of me?" What would happen if the next time we found ourselves stressed out and overwhelmed, we turned to our Source for guidance by asking, "Essence of All That Is, what do you want of me?"

It's a little less scary if we remember two things. First, we are the Beloved of God. Just as you wouldn't ask something awful of your own child, neither would God ask us to do something like move to Timbuktu. Second, I believe that God only desires what is in our highest good and in the best interest of everyone concerned.

So, go ahead . . . ask. Then listen. Listen longer and harder. Hear. Stand up. Take a step. Go!

LISTENING TO YOUR LIFE

*"Listen to your life. See it for the fathomless mystery it
is. In the boredom and pain of it, no less than in the
excitement and gladness: touch, taste, smell your way to
the holy and hidden heart of it, because in the last analysis
all moments are key moments, and life itself is grace."*
~ Frederick Buechner

When we think of listening, we think of hearing
with our ears, but I haven't found that to typically be
the case with the Spirit. I "heard" my call to ministry
twenty-eight years ago in words, but I heard it within
me, perhaps within my heart. It's sort of hard to
explain. That hasn't happened to me but a handful
of times. More often, I have "listened" to the Spirit
by watching for messages around me, or by paying
attention to my intuition.

When I was deciding about coming out and
leaving the United Methodist Church, I implored

God constantly to help me know what to do. One day, I spent the night with a friend (also clergy), and we spent much time talking about my situation and what I should do. When we got in her car in the garage the next morning, there was a small snakeskin lying on the passenger side windshield. It was simply amazing. I knew that the snake was a symbol of the Divine Feminine, and it was also a clear message about shedding an old skin that didn't fit anymore. Of course, I kept questioning and struggling for a while anyways.

All I can suggest is for you to open your mind and heart and pay attention. If a person comes to your mind out of the blue, contact them! If you feel compelled to go somewhere or try something, do it. Learn to know yourself well enough to know when it is your intuition speaking, or whether you have indigestion or you're projecting or making something up!

There is nothing quite like the feeling of working with the Universe as we walk through our days.

RIVER OF GOD

Here's something I don't claim to have any absolute answers about (well, that's true about a lot of things, actually . . .), but I do have some thoughts about it at a time like this: prayer. As always, feel free to take or leave my ponderings.

How we understand prayer has to do with how we understand God. There are plenty of folks out there who equate God with some kind of genie in the sky just waiting to be asked to grant wishes. And if you ask tenaciously enough and specifically enough, and if you've been faithful enough, The Great Genie God will grant your request. For me, the Divine is (and here is where words fail) more like an underlying river of love flowing through all things, always there, always available to be tapped into for strength, patience, direction, hope, courage, joy, compassion, and healing (I mean this more on a spiritual level than a physical level).

Prayer, then, is a way to intentionally connect with God, to dip our toes in the river for a few moments. Then, in our prayer of stillness or conversation or music or simple awareness of beauty or loving thoughts sent to someone else (however we choose to pray, there are many, many ways), we release our love and energy to mix with God's creative energy, and the energy of all Creation. Through that connection, we can draw the spiritual support we need, and I trust that if we're sending spiritual support to one another, the river is carrying it there.

If nothing else, prayer helps us to center, to be calmer, to remember that we are not alone and to focus on what is important.

PRAYER CHANGES US

There was a viral photo in March 2020 of two paramedics who worked together in Israel, Avraham Mintz and Zoher Abu Jama, using a small break in their busy day to pray. Mintz, a devout Jewish believer, donned his prayer shawl and faced Jerusalem. Abu Jama, an observant Muslim, rolled out his prayer rug and knelt the opposite direction, facing Mecca.

This brings me hope. It reminds me of a story about Mother Teresa, who was caring for a dying Indian man when she said to him, "You pray in your way, and I'll pray in my way, and together it will be beautiful."

Over three million people worldwide have died from COVID-19. Prayer is one way to be in solidarity with one another, regardless of the name you use for God or the words you use or the direction you face. And there is so much to pray for – the health and well-being of everyone, for those who are unemployed, our first responders and health-care workers, those who are grieving, and those currently fighting the virus . . . I could go on and on.

Sometimes I wonder what good prayer can do, if anything. Then I tell myself to trust how prayer changes us. When we pray (whatever this looks like for you), we ground ourselves again in Something More; we look beyond ourselves and recognize the connection we have with all of creation. This simple practice can soften our hearts, remind us to seek understanding, and lift us out of our cynicism and frustration (for a few moments, anyway). Maybe the biggest change of all is how prayer focuses us on a desire for life to be saner, simpler, safer, and far more spiritual.

Praying sends the much-needed energy of love and compassion out into the world, and I have a feeling this makes more difference than we know.

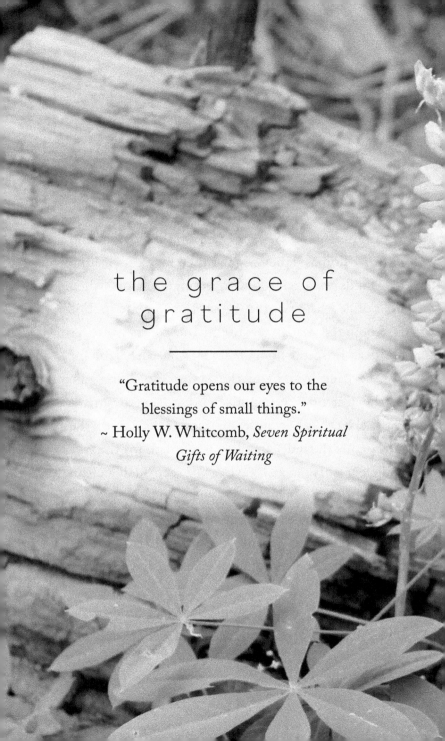

the grace of
gratitude

"Gratitude opens our eyes to the
blessings of small things."
~ Holly W. Whitcomb, *Seven Spiritual
Gifts of Waiting*

ON NOTICE

In his book, *Sermon Sparks*, theologian and pastor, Thomas Troeger, tells the story of washing his hands in a restroom in a small airport when he noticed it was the most immaculate public restroom he had ever used. The floors were as clean as hospital floors. Out of the corner of his eye, he caught sight of the janitor polishing one of the mirrors, eyeing his work to make sure it was perfect. When he came face to face with the janitor, he blurted, "Thank you so much for the way you clean this place. I have never seen such a clean restroom."

The man looked at him with tears springing to his eyes and said, "Thank you for noticing. No one has ever thanked me in all the years I have worked here."

It seems such a little thing, but every time I walk into Pick 'n Save, I thank the employee whose sole job for the day is to clean off the cart handles with disinfectant. It must be a boring, thankless job, and I can't imagine doing it for eight hours straight. So, I thank them for helping to keep everyone a bit safer.

Saying "thank you" doesn't take much, and it goes such a long way in boosting people's spirits and sense of self-worth. Too often the people closest to us are the most taken for granted. So, find the time. Thank the people in your family. Thank your partner, your children, your parents for all the little things they do for you, for the house, for your family. It doesn't take much – a pat on the back, a few kind words, a hug, or go all out and pick up some flowers or a nice bottle of wine *just because*.

And, while you're at it, remember to thank the Essence of All That Is for life, for this day, for another chance to grow, for sunlight and rain, for food, shelter, rest, work, friends . . . for all of it.

THE WORK IS THE MIRACLE

I lived with a sore neck for a long time. It got out of whack somehow (I'm blaming the pull lawnmower and/or the dog), and nothing I did seemed to help. It would be better some days, but then I'd go to sleep and wake up all messed up again. It's just wrong when sleep hurts you.

Finally, I said enough is enough and took myself to the chiropractor. Now, I'd tried this once or twice before, but the fix never stuck. I spent maybe ten months just dealing with the pain because I didn't want to spend the time, energy, or money to deal with it. Ignoring the pain did not make it go away. This time, I committed to seeing Dr. Kathy consistently until my neck was better. And you know what? My neck finally got better. Imagine that.

Not my finest moment, but if I don't learn something from it, then I just wasted all that pain and suffering for nothing. Why do we put off doing what is good for us? Why do we live with brokenness (mental, physical, and spiritual) for so long without doing what it takes to heal ourselves? Why lose days, weeks, maybe even years to the pain of broken relationships, health issues, and emotional baggage that weigh us down, instead of taking care of ourselves and reaping the benefits? Are we afraid to do the work? Are we afraid to heal? Are we afraid to let go of the pain? Are we hesitant to spend the money, as if investing in our health isn't a priority? Or, are we just plain lazy?

Living a life of wholeness is work. Sorry. It means taking care of our physical bodies through exercise, eating well, and seeing doctors, dentists, chiropractors, acupuncturists, or whoever when we need to. It means healing relationships by saying "I'm sorry," or "I forgive you," or "Let's talk about this." Living a life of wholeness means dealing with our emotional baggage and working through our grief, anger, shame, and pain – maybe even seeing a therapist! Living a life of wholeness means working through any God or church issues we may have so we can feel lighter, happier, healthier, and more whole.

No, it's not always fun or easy, but life is short and shouldn't be wasted. The sooner we do it, the more we'll be able to live life more abundantly.

A CRITICAL CHOICE

How are we doing? I know all this isolating and staying at home is getting old. It's hard not to feel sluggish, down, and even unmotivated. I get it. I have my moments, too.

This sounds cliché-ish, but it's true – the perfect antidote is gratitude. Every great spiritual tradition encourages gratitude, and when I practice being grateful, it is obvious why it is so important to our spiritual and mental health. When I focus on all the things and people I have to be grateful for, it gets me out of myself, my "poor me," frustration, annoyance, grumpiness, whatever, and fills me with light. It makes me wonder why I let myself live any other way.

We have a choice about where to focus our energy. Will we focus on the fear and worry, or will we focus on the positive, being grateful for the small things even when the big things are out of our control? Even on days when the news continues to be discouraging and I worry about the state of our world, I can still be grateful for a hot cup of tea and homemade scone, for a hot shower, my dog curled up beside me, and my great home office with all of my favorite things. I can also be thankful for you, my readers, who give me cause to reflect and write and share.

There is so much that is good in life. It doesn't mean I ignore what is difficult. I am aware and informed, but when I choose to put my energy into being grateful and finding positive ways to live, everyone (at least in my house) is better for it.

What are you grateful for? Where will you focus your energy today?

TO DIE LAUGHING

Twenty-four years ago, I gave birth to my second son, Samuel. I was in seminary and hoping he'd come a little earlier to get me out of midterm exams. No such luck. Actually, I was hoping he'd arrive any day *but* April Fools' Day. The joke was on me. You see, for some strange reason, I was worried his life would be plagued with bad jokes about his birthday . . . Gratefully, it hasn't really been an issue.

It probably shouldn't have bothered me at all, because humor is one of the greatest gifts of being human. A good laugh is good for the soul and good for our physical well-being. Of all the people I interact with, I have the hardest time with people who have no sense of humor, who barely ever crack a smile. Frankly, I feel sort of bad for them. What a sad way to live, never to feel the levity of laughter or to laugh until you cry at something completely ridiculous. Can you remember the last time you did that? Those are holy moments!

We have a few signs around our house that make me smile every time I look at them. One in the living room says, "Come to the dark side, we have cookies." And there is one hanging on the front door that says, "Ring the bell, win a dog!" (I really do love our dog, but there are days . . .)

When we die laughing, the only things that actually do die or come to an end, even for a moment, are our anxiety and worry and fear. A good laugh can make our day, or at least restore its sanity.

I know these are serious times, but we need to maintain some sense of humor to get through them. I'm so very grateful to have people around me who are willing to laugh with me and at me (when appropriate)! Tell a joke today. Smile. Laugh. Let the Spirit play in you by doing so.

THE WASTE OF WORRY

Mark Twain once said, "My life has been filled with many misfortunes, most of which never happened."

This thought is right up there with the concept that worrying must work, since most of what we worry about never happens! I hope most of you aren't letting your minds run the hamster wheels of worry, fear, and what-ifs. Yet, from what I see on Facebook, many people are losing sleep, eating poorly, and lacking motivation. I get it. I do. My daughter got a low-grade fever early on in this pandemic, and something that was once not such a big deal was a bit alarming. She was and is fine, by the way.

We often don't care to believe this, but the reality is that the majority of us *choose* to get on the hamster wheel. It may not feel like it, but unless we're struggling with depression or anxiety, we do. We can also *choose* to get off by living in the moment, by looking for the blessings that surround us and being grateful, and by finding positive things to do. The movie *Eat, Pray, Love* had a great suggestion for how to handle grief, worry, and concern for someone we're not with. It's as simple as this: when you think of them, send them love and light. Sometimes I add a candle to that. For me, I feel like envisioning them enveloped in that wonderful, positive energy of love and warmth is much better than sending the anxious energy of our worrying.

To take my own advice . . . this moment on the couch with my tea, my cookie, and my dog curled up against me as I watch the rain and write to you, is really good. I am so grateful for my life, my family, my home, and for an amazing spiritual community.

SPIRITUALITY OF ABUNDANCE

People live in fear of not having enough. Do you remember the early days of the pandemic when all you had to do was go to the grocery store to see how people bought in – hook, line, and sinker – to the belief that there will not be enough to go around. Spiritually, this energy of scarcity takes us down a very unhealthy road. It is a contractive, fear-based, anxiety-ridden energy that fuels selfishness, greed, and toilet paper hoarding. This type of panic is a breeding ground for craziness. We all need to take a collective breath.

A spirituality of abundance asks us to see what we have, not what we don't have. I have a feeling that all of us have a few weeks' worth of food in our homes, roofs over our heads, money in the bank, friends and family who care and whom we can rely on. Oh, we don't *want* to rely on anyone – heaven forbid we have to ask for help – but that is part of our abundance.

We're not alone, so let's be grateful and accepting of it. If you run out of toilet paper (or whatever), you have lots of people you can ask to lend you a roll or two!

Maybe, think of it this way. By every standard in the world, we have more than most. This is at the root of greed: a seed of not appreciating when enough is, indeed, enough.

Deep breath. Let's count our proverbial blessings, be grateful for the people we can count on (even if we don't want to), and recognize that we have enough (and some to share).

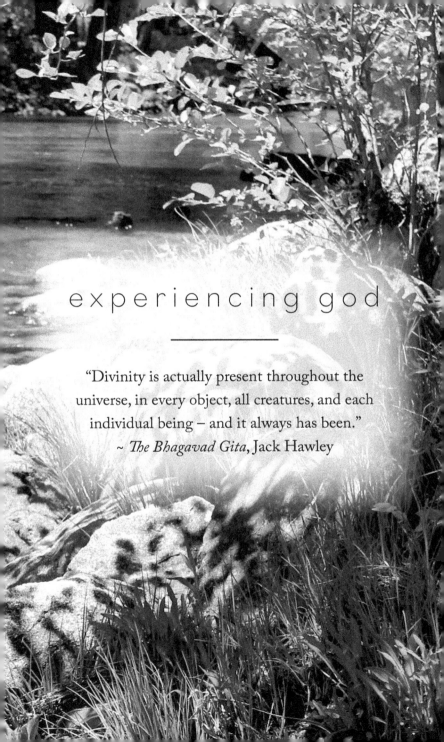

experiencing god

"Divinity is actually present throughout the
universe, in every object, all creatures, and each
individual being – and it always has been."
~ *The Bhagavad Gita*, Jack Hawley

LIMITLESS GOD

Recently, when I googled "experiencing God" all I got were images of someone's book with that title and the picture of an old white guy with a beard on the cover.

Now, I'm sorry – if this is your thing, that's fine, but you can stop reading here. Are they (the three male authors) trying to tell everyone *this* is the God we are supposed to experience? How many experiences of God have they discredited or disqualified simply with that cover? How many people will read their book and miss God because the image of God they're supposed to be experiencing has been limited? If a picture paints one thousand words, then this one excludes thousands more. Sorry, again . . . I guess I'm ranting.

To experience the Divine, we need to fling the door wide open to the possibilities before us. Many people don't think of God as any sort of actual deity, but more so as a potent energy of love, grace, possibilities, hope, joy, comfort, strength, gentleness, courage, and more. For others, the Holy One is Spirit, Breath, or Wind which breathes life into dead bones, stirs the flames of courage, speaks in soft whispers, and takes us places we'd never imagine. The Essence of All That Is can be found in the twinkle of an eye, a belly laugh, a sigh too deep for words, an anguished cry, the innocent wonder of a child, and more. And more. And more! In anything . . . everything . . . there is a spark of the Divine waiting to be acknowledged, to be touched and tasted, heard and held, basked in and gazed at, quieted by and aroused by.

There is also nothing wrong with personifying God for ourselves. Hindus have, metaphorically speaking, 33 million (or 330 million, depending on who you talk to) gods and goddesses, reminding us that the Divine has countless faces, but one essence underlying all of them. Perhaps trying on a different "face" for God would help us to experience God differently.

Untying the Strong Woman, by Clarrisa Pinkola Estes, gives permission to see Mother Mary as more than the obedient, docile, milk-toast Mary of the Catholic Church. Estes brings her alive into a Mother Goddess in her own right. For Estes (and for many people, Hispanics especially), Mary is also the Great Mother who is experienced in the corn, food, and earth that nourishes. She is Wind, Fire, Warrior, Heart of Gold, and One Who Knows. She is Mother of the Conquered, pouring out strength to those who are oppressed. For Estes, she is the girl gang leader in heaven who "calls for those broken to walk as warriors . . . to enact her holy heart by unfurling the ancient virtues of strength and sheltering, speaking up, standing up, taking action, and creating works in her name and in that of the God of Love she brought to Earth."

In these challenging times, our souls yearn for the one-on-one experience of the Divine more than ever. So, let's not just fling open that door to new possibilities. Let's tear the blasted thing off its rusty hinges and release ourselves from the God of "Limited Images."

GOD IS NOT A MICROMANAGER

I heard recently of a thirty-year-old young man who lost his father when he was fourteen years old, and he has never forgiven God for it. From what I understand, this is most likely a result of growing up with a mother who pushed religion on him and professed belief in an almighty, all-powerful God (who would probably look poorly on him if he did something wrong, like not go to church).

This saddens and frustrates me, because believing in this God is a recipe for disaster. If God is truly all-powerful and we pray for someone to be cured but they aren't, or if someone dies tragically in an accident or something else awful happens, then we question why God would let that happen. Why doesn't this great God, who supposedly loves everyone, stop all the bad things in the world from happening? And if God could prevent these things but for some mysterious reason chooses not to, then of course I'm pissed at God for letting something bad happen to someone I love.

We have a great cartoon painting by Jerry Belland in our living room. It is Jesus and God playing chess, and it is entitled "What Jesus and God Do All Day in Heaven." Jesus is pondering over a move out loud, "Hmmm. That means Ellie is screwed!" And God says, while moving a little figure, "OK. I'm gonna kill Charlie off over here then move Paula over here." Is this really what people mean when they say, "God must have a reason for this"?

To me, this is spiritually abusive theology, implying that we have a capricious God who dispassionately takes people out. Nope. Doesn't work for me. God is not a micromanager or a genie granting wishes or a chess master playing with people's lives.

God is the strength to go on when we feel like we can't. God is the courage to stand firm in the face of oppression. God is love shared with those who are lonely. God is the dog or cat who comforts you. God is the awakening of our souls to see a bigger picture where all are one. God is forgiveness that brings healing. God is laughter that lightens our souls. God is the spark of hope that can't be quenched. God is the presence in which our souls rest and find peace.

If you prefer your God to be an all-powerful genie, fine with me, but I simply can't do the mental gymnastics to make that work.

DARKNESS AND LIGHT

True confessions . . . there are days when I don't know if I want to laugh or cry, and I will occasionally do both. Some days, I am torn between missing all of the people in my life and all the things we used to be able to do, and yet also enjoying this time of slowing down and being home.

I guess this is life. We live in the constant tension between life and death, sweet and bitter, darkness and light, joy and grief, dancing and mourning. Some days this is easier than others. The author of *Ecclesiastes* reminds us of this in the famous passage that says there is a season for everything under the sun . . . a time to plant and reap, to be born and to die, to laugh and weep, to tear and mend, to embrace and refrain from embracing . . . (Nailed that last one, didn't they?)

And where is the Divine in all this? Right there in the midst of it. God is not a static noun, a thing looking on from afar. God is a verb: action and movement. God is the constant, generative, creative energy undergirding all of life. God is in our courage to keep going, the comfort we offer one another, the challenge to grow. God is love, compassion, grace, integrity, and hope.

This creative movement is within us, and we are within it – always.

SIZE MATTERS

Last week, I came across an interesting quote by Alfred Korzybski, an American-Polish mathematician and philosopher who said, "The map is not the territory." The spiritual extrapolation of this might be, "The Bible is not God" or, "The Church is not God." I've had to remind myself of this last one quite a few times over the years. Church organizations, clergy, and people in churches do many, many manipulative, unkind, unloving, and judgmental things. It has been more than enough to turn scores of people away from religion. Personally, I've had my fair share of doubts about continuing as a pastor at times. Then I remind myself that *the church is NOT God!*

In my humble opinion, one of humanity's biggest mistakes when it comes to religion is to believe that God can be captured in a set of words or doctrine. Then people decide that their words are the only right words to describe God, or a doctrine is the one right way to worship and believe in God. How silly! If God can be contained by a book or a set of rules, then clearly this God is too small!

I *always* feel inadequate when trying to describe the Divine or preach about the Essence of All That Is. How can I possibly accurately represent a Divine One that is so much greater than my limited comprehension? Frankly, for God to be God, then He/She/It *must* (again, in my humble opinion) be bigger than I can comprehend, with a love far purer than mine will ever be, and possess an unparalleled amount of compassion, grace, and forgiveness.

When God becomes racist, homophobic, sexist, hung up on rules, and wants to send people to hell, we know for certain that we've created God in our own image.

ZERO CONDITIONS

"God is love."

This simple, profound statement found in the New Testament book of *1 John*, seems to have been forgotten and replaced with "God is love, but . . ." or "God is love, unless . . ." This God of "buts" and "unlesses" appears to have been created in humanity's image, an image in which love is conditional based upon another's behavior, beliefs, skin color, political view, or whatever. Consequently, "God is love" morphed into God is king, God is judge or God is the law. Most people can't even *conceive* of a God who is able to love unconditionally, wastefully, and boundlessly, because is it so hard for us to love that way ourselves!

The author of *1 John* also says, ". . . everyone who loves is begotten of God and has knowledge of God." This is more than love between friends; this is different than erotic love; this is much deeper than, "I love chocolate." This love sees past people's mistakes, looks deeper than differences, and sees the hurtful things we have said or done as not being part of our authentic selves. However, oh my, this love is hard to find when faced with ignorance, violence, prejudice, meanness, and selfishness.

I suspect the reason we have had only a handful of really bright, shining spiritual leaders like Jesus, Mother Teresa, and Desmond Tutu in our history is because loving unconditionally is just so damn difficult. Here's something I often do to help me think and behave more lovingly (because occasionally I've wanted to string some folks up by their toenails) – I try to be generous in my assumptions. For example, if I'm getting annoyed at someone driving too slowly, I try to reflect on it in a gentler way. Like, maybe they were in a car accident and are somewhat afraid to drive. Or maybe they are older, and I would want someone to be kind to me when I get old. Or maybe they don't really know what the speed limit is or aren't sure where they are going. Does this make sense? Well, it seems to help me, anyway.

I guess the bottom line is . . . *GIVE PEOPLE THE BENEFIT OF THE DOUBT.*

God is love. When we love purely, without conditions or limitations, is when we truly show that we know God.

WHEN FAITH FAILS

So, here's a tough one . . . what if our faith fails? Maybe you're one of the lucky ones, and this has never happened to you, but I am confident that not everyone is so fortunate.

Faith never fails when life is good, our blessings are numerous and obvious, and the world appears to be full of glorious possibilities for the future. At times like these, we're either thanking the Divine for so much goodness, or we've sort of forgotten about God because, well, life is so good – what did we need God for?

Faith fails when we get slapped upside the head by life and find things careening out of control. There is some crazy statistic like 98% of people who visit a church for the first time have had some kind of major life change or crisis within the last year. My gut says they are looking for a place which will shore up their bruised or damaged faith, or maybe more specifically, they are looking for a God they can have faith in. You see, I have to wonder if our faith sometimes fails because we set God up to fail by expecting way too much of God and too little of ourselves.

For example, if God doesn't save someone from death, or restore a struggling relationship, or erase our grief, or fix someone's mental illness, or keep us from losing our job, then maybe there really isn't a God. *Maybe God just doesn't care.* Worse: *Maybe God just doesn't care about me.* Do you see how this thought process goes in circles?

Yes, my faith has wavered over the years, but as I've evolved in my understanding of God, my faith has grown stronger. God didn't give my mother cancer when I was a teenager. God didn't turn people against me. God didn't create our puppy Rosie with underdeveloped kidneys. God didn't give my daughter a heart condition. God didn't send this pandemic. And God is not a genie that fixes everything that I want fixed the way I want it (or them) fixed.

For me, God is an energy of Love that, when tapped into, is enough to guide me through most anything with grace and integrity. God is the Ground of My Being that strengthens, supports, and nourishes me through life. God is the deepest Essence of my True Self, found under layers of baggage and ego. God is Light that helps me find the positive, the possibilities, and the hope in difficult situations. God is Presence in the warmth of the sun, the freshness of the wind, and the kindness of others. In all this, I have faith.

GOD IS NOT LOST

Christian tradition tells us that at the end of Jesus' life, after going through a week of hell – rejection, betrayal, beatings, humiliation, and the incomprehensible pain of crucifixion – he cried out from the cross, "My God, my God, why have you forsaken me?" Honestly, I *so* love Jesus for this moment. No wonder he cried out. To dedicate one's life to sharing the love of God in compassion and justice and then come to this kind of end would make anyone wonder if they'd gotten it all wrong. In any case, it was in this moment that Jesus became most like us.

You know, this line is actually a quote from *Psalm 22:1*, written by David, who cried out from his own place of despair. We've all been there. We've felt so bereft, empty, lost, alone, humiliated, scared, devastated, broken, and confused that we felt surely God must have turned heel and walked out the door.

Yet, I believe in my heart of hearts that the Divine never forsakes us. It just feels like it when our pain overwhelms us. If God is the Very Essence of Love, and if the spark of the Divine is in *all* things, then it is *impossible*, by definition, for us to ever truly be separated from God, no matter how much it feels that way. Even in the times of our greatest suffering, I trust that the Spirit is working within us and around us to help us get through. If getting through just isn't possible, then I believe we are held gently while we make the transition to whatever adventure awaits us after this life.

Where is God? Everywhere. All of the time. Eternally. Just stop, look, and listen. Just pay attention. Just take note. All is well.

the wisdom
to wave the
white flag

————————

"Try something different. Surrender."
~ Rumi

SURRENDER

As much as I try to remain centered, calm, and optimistic, I still get overwhelmed sometimes. And when I feel a bit in over my head, I become tense, anxious, short-tempered, and like Blanche Devereaux once said, "I'm wound up tighter than a girdle on a Baptist minister›s wife at an all-you-can-eat pancake breakfast!»

The problem is that even though I feel crazed, I still feel like I have to push through and push hard. However, most of my work involves some type of spiritual creativity, which does *not* respond well to pushing. The more I want to clamp down, and the more I worry about not being able to do it, the more I can't do it, and it becomes a self-fulfilling prophecy.

What I *need* to do is what I least *want* to do. Surrender. Go with the flow. Recognize that wanting to push through is my ego's way of saying, "I'm in control, I'll do it myself." Surrender says, "I'm completely kidding myself if I think I'm in control. I'm releasing my near-death grip and relaxing into the Divine Flow, trusting something other than my puny, freaked-out brain."

I almost didn't write about this because I either sound like I'm losing it or I'm bragging. I assure you, neither are the case. This is just darn hard stuff, which is why I'm trying valiantly to write something coherent about it.

Surrender takes a deep breath and an opening to the universe. Surrender shuts down the constrictive fight-or-flight response when I'm afraid I'm going to let myself or someone else down. Surrender calms and assures and waits and believes. Surrender offers all of oneself in service to the Universal One. And when my ego starts squeaking in the background about getting everything done, I have to calmly tell it that I'm not listening – also easier said than done.

Perhaps this beautiful prayer of surrender, (slightly adapted) written by Anglican Bishop Lancelot Andrewes at the turn of the seventeenth century, will help today:

"Essence of Life that flows through all things,
I give you my hands to do your work.

I give you my feet to go your way.
I give you my eyes to see as you do.
I give you my tongue to speak your words.
I give you my mind that you may think in me.
I give you my spirit that you may pray in me.
I give you my heart that you may love in me.
I give you my whole self that you may grow in me.
May it be so."

FINGER KISSING

I don't like to make mistakes (not that it happens very often, mind you), but when I do, I excel at beating myself up over them. I know all too well that I'm not perfect and never will be. I've tried to get better about forgiving myself and being compassionate with myself, because being perfect isn't the goal. The goal is learning and growing, but I forget this sometimes.

Violinist Stephen Nachmanovitch, in his book *The Art of Is*, tells a great story about giving a series of workshops on improvisation at Julliard. One group of students did amazingly well and eventually worked their way up to two amazing pieces of improvisational music. Then they played a third piece where they were out of sync and out of tune with one another. During the discussion of that last piece, the young musicians were really hard on themselves, feeling guilty that they hadn't done better. They were expecting Nachmanovitch to berate their miserable piece. Instead, to their surprise, he had them put down their instruments and walk around the room kissing their fingertips, contemplating and appreciating all ten of them.

Nachmanovitch wrote, "Kissing your fingers is a radical, transformative practice. It is not pretense that everything is good or that our mistakes don't matter. They do matter. Finger-kissing is rather a celebration of our personal participation in the immense moment-to-moment labor of learning and evolution."

The spiritual path challenges us to fully engage in this transformative practice called life. Stopping to put ourselves down, wallow in guilt, or drown in anger toward ourselves or others effectively squashes any possibility for transformation.

Perhaps today we should kiss our fingertips, expressing gratitude toward ourselves for continuing to risk putting ourselves into the fray of this beautiful, crazy, mixed-up, awesome world. Perhaps today we can embrace our ability to learn and grow from our mistakes, gradually evolving into the persons we were created to be.

WU WEI

I'll admit it. I'm not only a leader, I'm also a fixer. I recognize that I can also have a fairly strong personality (I believe a high school friend once called me bossy). So, I try to be very careful not to get in the way of my own spiritual growth (not to mention that of others) because I think I know what is best. Unintentionally forcing or manipulating our agendas in any given situation is not healthy. The best way to live in alignment with the energy of God, the great Tao master Lao Tzu once said, is to get our egos out of the way, to move with the rhythms of life, and never violate the needs and harmony of human beings in the process.

When we are exhausted from trying to fix our lives or fix others or make things happen the way we want them to, it is time to learn the practice of *wu wei*. With wu wei, the action of nonaction, we allow ourselves to stop long enough for God to begin to fill us up and work with the pieces of our lives in a natural, noncoercive way. From this position of waiting, observing, and awareness, we will be able to recognize where the Spirit is moving in our lives to help us grow or to help us know the next best step to take. It is then that *all is done without doing*.

I've always been in awe of people who know how to sail. They seem to effortlessly harness the wind to take them where they want to go. The opposite of this happened when we went sailing with my brother and his wife and son in the San Diego Bay. Actually, we were doing pretty well until we sailed too close to an island and got stuck in the sandy bottom. Have you ever tried to push a sailboat? It's not easy or fun. So, wu wei is like catching the wind. Not utilizing wu wei is like pushing the sailboat.

Wu wei requires trust in the Essence of All That Is. Trust that we are loved and understood deeply. Trust that we don't need to force our agenda for life to turn out well. Trust that if we take a deep breath and allow things to simply be for a bit, we will be able to see the Spirit at work around us. Then as we notice this, we will feel stronger and less tired. We will find that we are now moving with the Spirit, instead of trying to make the Spirit move with us.

THE LONGING FOR LESS

Theologian Meister Eckhart once said, "God is not found in the soul by adding anything but by subtracting." It seems to me that this is true.

In my humble opinion, religion has often asked people to add all kinds of beliefs and practices to their lives in order to find God. It's become a list of hoops one must jump through or a ladder one must climb. If you go to worship, give money, confess your sins, believe the right way, read scripture, serve at the food pantry, pray daily, receive communion, behave the right way, and so on and so on . . . then God will reward you, bless you, and save you. You aren't even promised to *find* God or to *know* God, because that hasn't been the goal. Forgive my cynicism here, but the goal was to keep you coming back, giving money, and perpetuating the institution.

Now, that's not to say that you *can't* experience God at a religious service, but religious institutions don't want you to know that God can also be found without their help. In fact, knowing God in the depths of one's soul is an interior journey which entails stripping away our belief that we ever needed an intermediary person or practice to reach God. Instead, it requires peeling away the layers of baggage covering our authentic selves in anger, grudges, shame, guilt, fear, and lack of self-esteem. It requires removing the desire to judge or blame or exclude others. It requires letting go of the concept of duality: us and them, mine and theirs, good and bad, spirit and flesh, mind and body, God and humans, light and dark, and so on.

When we've subtracted all these things and are left with our most bare, vulnerable, true selves, it is then that we also find the Divine within.

IMPROV

This is dating me, but I think it was Hannibal Smith from *The A-Team* who said, "I love it when a plan comes together." This is what we want (myself included): for all things to run perfectly and to do so *all* the time. Taken to the extreme, it is this need that creates micromanagers, bridezillas, control freaks, and we've-never-done-it-that-way-before (therefore we can't do anything new now) folks.

But life just doesn't work that way. Stephen Nachmanovitch, in his book *The Art of Is*, says, "Improvising is life itself," and, "Come prepared, but be willing to accept interruptions and invitations." We do the best we can do but allow ourselves to be flexible and roll with the changes without getting too stressed, angry, or frustrated. This is easier said than done, sometimes. But if our mantra became, "Life is improvising," how might that change our response to those things that derail our planning?

Honestly, I've found that there can be true power in improvising. When we hold a tight rein, it doesn't give the Spirit room to move, and we risk missing potentially wonderful things. Preaching off a manuscript is like that for me. I used a written sermon when I was first starting off, but now I find that even when I use it to cheat a little, I become stiff and too formal because the message can't flow where it needs to. Mind you, I prepare like crazy now, but then I say a prayer right before I preach that I'll be open enough to be a conduit for the Spirit. Please God, don't let me get in the way! Some of my best sermons have had more improv than you realize.

By definition, you can't plan improv. There is a level of trust and faith – in our own creativity and in the Spirit – which develops over time. When I'm stuck trying to write a sermon, I often remind myself that God hasn't let me down yet. Then I mentally sit on the nagging fear that whispers, "What if this is the first time?"

I know all of us have had plans interrupted and probably faced all kinds of different challenges during this pandemic. But I also see so many amazing ways people are improvising and finding meaningful, productive ways to continue on.

INTENTIONAL WHINING

I'm sorry, but some days I get downright whiny. I've had enough of social distancing. I miss everyone. I miss hugs and having meetings in person. I'm tired of gray, cold and dreary mornings, and I don't want to walk the dog. I don't want to think about viruses or how long this will last. I'm tired of making dinner, and I don't like wearing a mask any more than anyone else. I'm tired of watching what I eat so I don't come out of this twenty pounds heavier. I don't want to talk on the phone; I want to meet for coffee and a cinnamon scone from Panera. Sigh.

We started Whiny Thursday years ago when the kids were in high school. It seemed to make sense to have a day to just let loose and get all the whininess out. Then the rest of the week, if anyone started to whine, we reminded them that they had to wait for Thursday! This significantly curtailed whining in our home, even on Thursdays, oddly enough. We still do it even now that the kids are grown and mostly moved out.

How does this tie into spirituality? Well, spirituality isn't about denying the tougher emotions, but rather about processing them and working through them. So, perhaps it's spiritual to hold space on one day for our whininess. Otherwise known as: name it . . . claim it . . . embrace it . . . and then let it go.

I'm not entirely sure why this works, but intentionally whining seems to take the sting out of it. Whining when you're *allowed* to whine almost isn't any fun. With the passion taken out of it, we tend let it go easier. Weird, I know. But once I've gotten it out, I can move on to more positive ways to spend my time. This is probably why talk therapy works. Go ahead, try it.

TRUSTING GOD

Just before Jesus died, he uttered these words, "Abba, into your hands I commit my spirit."

I feel like committing our spirits to the Divine Essence is easier in death than it is in life. Sure, we all fight death with everything we have, but when it comes to the end, most people are ready to release the pain and struggle of this world and dwell once again in the embrace of the Spirit.

If we trust God at that point, why can't we trust God a bit more during our lives? Any talk about surrendering or letting go is taken as a nice concept, but unrealistic. It pretty much goes against everything we've been taught. We want *control* over our lives ... or at least the illusion of control. We'd never admit it, but I think most of us believe that we can do a better job with our lives than God can.

As a general rule, our culture is wildly opposed to *surrender*. We must win at all costs, personally and collectively. This is also why people abhor asking for or seeking help of any kind.

Spiritually, I think people fear that if they "surrender" to the Divine, they'll end up as missionaries, eating locusts and using outhouses! For me, surrender looks more like getting on a blow-up chair (with a drink holder, mind you) and floating down the river, instead of walking upstream against the current. Surrender means listening for the still, small voice to point me in the right direction. Surrender means doing the best I can and then trusting the Spirit to take it from there. Surrender means not always having all the answers or certainty in my life, but to trust the journey. Surrender means letting go of my ego and embracing compassion and love. Surrender means opening the door and letting the Divine come in and rearrange the furniture, and being surprised by how much I like the change! I could go on, but hopefully you get the drift. I'm not always good at it, but life is better when I am.

Jesus didn't just commit his spirit in death, but also every day of his life. How about this . . . just for today, I commit my spirit to the Essence of All That Is, trusting that Love will lead me well.

FORGIVENESS

Have you ever been betrayed? Or treated unfairly? Have you ever been crucified (metaphorically) because you spoke truth to power or stood up for the underdog? I have, and let me tell you, forgiveness wasn't exactly rolling off my lips.

When I'm in my hurt place, I want to lash out in anger, hoping to make some very salient points about how right I was and how wrong "they" were, maybe even tossing in some pain and humiliation for good measure (not pretty, not proud of that, but honest anyway). However, when I'm in my more enlightened, connected, and grounded place, I feel completely different. From this much better spiritual place, I can remember that there is a deeper reality beneath the surface of our grasping egos, our physical desires, and our emotional neediness.

From this place of spiritual enlightenment, connected to the unconditional love of God, I can more easily offer forgiveness, because I am better able to see how others let their fears and their egos run the show. I don't want to make forgiveness sound like flipping a light switch. I recognize that forgiveness is often incremental, a process that may stall or speed ahead. It may require laying fallow or a leap of faith.

The challenge for us when we are hurt or when we've been stepped on, ridiculed, or betrayed is to take a deep breath and remember that all that really matters is living life with great love. Whoever has hurt us doesn't get that. And then we can let go, because our souls know all that crap won't last anyway. Love lasts. It is the universal energy of eternity, the essence of you and me and all that is.

I didn't say it was easy.

SACRED UNCERTAINTY

In times of crisis and change, one of the most difficult things to deal with is not knowing. Not knowing how long it will last. Not knowing what will happen next. Not knowing how we will manage. Yes, it's hard not knowing, but perhaps it is also a good time to practice letting go of the illusion of control, which can be a challenge for me, given that I'm a recovering control freak who tends to backslide a lot.

Part of the spiritual journey is trusting that the Spirit is in the midst of the chaos, working to bring goodness and light. We can see this in the multitude of ways people reach out to help and support one another.

When I'm successful at channeling this type of trust, there is a sense of *sacred uncertainty*. The waiting, the gap, the not knowing about the future – all become sacred in the presence of the Spirit. Sitting quietly with sacred uncertainty, I can smile and breathe again. Suddenly, my brain can take a break from all unanswered questions. Gradually, I feel more at peace and see more clearly what I might do to make the present moment a little better for myself and for others.

Sacred uncertainty means that every day we are living, we are also dying. We get up anyway. This is faith.

be still

———————

"Your innermost sense of self, of who you are,
is inseparable from stillness. This is the *I Am*
that is deeper than name and form."
~ Eckhart Tolle

PRACTICE PATIENCE

One of the ways I embraced "isolating" at home was by taking a watercolor class of sorts. My dad used to be a wonderful watercolor artist, and I've always loved the medium in general but never had the time or courage to try it.

I've discovered that watercolor painting requires a great deal of patience. While some people tell me that I have a lot of patience, I wouldn't include it on my top five attributes list. When painting in watercolor, I've learned that sometimes it is imperative to stop and let it dry when things start to go wrong. To me, this feels completely counterintuitive. When things start to look wrong, I want to fix it immediately, but the more I add water or paint, the worse it gets! The better bet would be to take a deep breath, let it dry, then look at it a little while later with fresh eyes and try again.

Life really isn't so different. Sometimes when I've screwed up, I want to push and push until it's better, fixed, healed. I can be the same way about a sermon, wanting to push through when I get writer's block or it isn't coming together well. Or there are times when my partner and I argue (not that we argue much), and I want to work it out immediately. It's hard to remember that some things just take time.

I've found much benefit in taking a deep breath and stepping back for perspective. I walk outside to check out my vegetable garden, make a snack, or just do something completely different for a bit. Some things even require a good night's sleep. This actually works in relationships, too, even though we often hear the phrase, "Don't go to bed angry." Agree to come back to the discussion after some sleep, a break, and hopefully finding a fresh perspective – but I digress.

Here's my point. Practice patience. Patience with ourselves. Patience with others. Sometimes solving the problems in our lives goes much better if we don't try to force something to be better instantaneously.

We need to move our egos over and make way for our souls. Patience is a lot like listening. Patience is shutting up so the Spirit can be heard.

YOU ARE THE CONDUIT

Here's my question of the day: *How do you experience God?* Note: this is a completely different question than *Who is God to you?* The second question is easily answered by regurgitating all the things you've been told about who or what the Divine Essence is. When I asked this question of a college class, most of the responses I received were obvious recitations of belief learned by rote in a mostly long-forgotten confirmation or Sunday School class.

On the other hand, *experiencing God* requires awareness, recognition, thought, and response. It amazes me how many people struggle to answer this question. Then again, the Church never really encouraged its people to think for themselves and trust their own connections. Instead, the institutional church has historically assigned Jesus, Mary, priests, pastors, and saints as go-betweens. If I only had a nickel for every time someone asked me to "talk to

the Big Guy" because I supposedly have a closer connection, or more pull or something. Well, I'd have
more than a few nickels, but you get my point.

How we experience God is a mystical question
asking us to risk sounding a little wacky by verbalizing
something intangible: we *feel* God, we *hear* God, we
see God, we *know* God.

Everyone's answers will likely be different because the Holy One can be experienced in an infinite
number of expansive, generous, ineffable, ordinary,
and extraordinary ways. But don't take my word for
it. Contrary to popular belief, I do not have a red
phone connected to the Divine on my office desk.
You are your own conduit!

Listen for the sound underneath the sound, the
invisible waves that touch all things, connect all
things, and create a harmony with the most unlikely
contributors. Jackhammers and birds and dogs barking
and planes and whispers all become expressions of
the One's sound which vibrates through all of life.

In stillness, *feel* below the surface of the everyday.
Close your eyes, relax your body, open your mind and
your hands, and feel the gentle, yet incredibly strong
stream of love, peace, and compassion that gives us

the courage to be true to our deepest, most authentic selves.

Know that you are loved fiercely by the very Essence of Love. How else could you have known how to love as fully as you have in your life? Look deep within, past the bumps and bruises, past the fears and insecurities, past your skeptical, critical, cynical self and know that you – *you* – are Beloved. This is the best possible experience of God.

BE GENTLE WITH YOURSELF

My son, Sam, called me one night during the first summer of the pandemic because he thought Mom could shed some light on the "funk" he was in. He'd had about four days when he didn't feel like getting up in the morning, didn't have the motivation to do his homework, didn't have the energy to work on some projects he had planned, and was just sort of blah.

He said he'd been eating well, forcing himself to exercise (even if he didn't feel like it), was getting out in the sunshine (even if just to sit there with the dog and soak up some vitamin D), was getting plenty of sleep, and had good things happening in his life. It just didn't make sense.

I told him lots of people are feeling the same way, and it seems to be a result of everything that is going on in the world. It's sort of a general malaise that creeps up on us when we least expect it. My suggestion to him was this: take a break, be gentle with yourself, sleep, do something you love, and allow yourself to just be with the feelings for a bit. If it lasts too long, then we have a different conversation to have, but you'll likely bounce back with some self-compassion and understanding.

Sam didn't like my answer. He's a doer. He wanted to *do* something to fix it. Now, I never do this with my kids, but I finally said, "Sam, you know there is a Bible story about this," (if you miss the reference, look up the story of Namaan in *2 Kings* 5). If I told you that all you needed to do was bike fifty miles and you'd be fine, you'd do it, but because I told you to go easy on yourself, you can't accept it! He got a good laugh and told me I was right (as mothers always are). He agreed to try it my way for a day or two.

If you're struggling with these sorts of feelings, understand that it's normal; it's part of the grieving we're all doing. Be kind to yourself. Sometimes trying to force our way through just makes things worse. So, hug yourself, kiss your fingertips, relax in the sunshine, have a good cry, listen to music that allows you to feel, hug your dog, talk to someone who will truly listen and empathize. I promise we'll get through this.

THE BLACK HOLE OF ANXIETY

One of the hardest pieces of advice in Scripture comes from *Matthew 6:34*, "Enough of worrying about tomorrow! Let tomorrow take care of itself. Today has troubles enough of its own."

Every time I've ever mentioned this passage, every control freak in the room goes ballistic. *That is ridiculous, we have to plan! We need to schedule appointments, make a list for the grocery store, get ready for a birthday party (or wedding, or whatever) and book plane tickets and a hotel for a trip. We can't just do everything in the spur of the moment!*

So, let's be clear. Planning and worrying are different. Scheduling and succumbing to the black hole of anxiety are different. Thinking ahead and living constantly in the future are different. Get it?

I usually take two long walks a day with the dog. Sometimes, my feet walk while my mind takes its own frenzied jaunt down worry lane. It makes me a little annoyed with myself. This time is supposed to be for spiritual sustenance, a chance to take a deep breath and enjoy some fresh air, maybe even hold my honey's hand and have a nice chat. But no . . . on these days, my brain hardly even accompanies me. I can take a forty-minute walk and miss the whole experience because I was worried about something I could do *nothing* about. Despite the seemingly popular belief that worrying works because most of the things we worry about never happen, worrying about tomorrow ad nauseam will steal today.

Whenever this happens, I vow to change my errant ways – I hope you'll join me. We can schedule what we need to, plan what we must, deal with the problems of *today* as they arise, and there will still be plenty of time left to live in the moment. No matter the state of the world, or life, there are always plenty of beautiful moments to live.

BEGINNING THE DAY

When I was younger, and especially when I had kids to get ready for school, I tended to hit the ground running as soon as I got out of bed. Now that I'm a tad bit older, though, I have the blessing of being able to ease into the day. I can have a cup of tea and a cookie while I watch the sunrise and read a spiritual book. I can take a deep breath and be still for a few moments, simply pausing in gratitude for another day.

How did you start your day? Did you jump straight into the news? (Not a terribly uplifting way to start off a day.) Did you open up Facebook to check the latest posts? Have you told someone you love them? Checked in with God?

When my daughter was five, she said, "Everyone has a heart because that is how God talks to us." That being the case (and I believe it is in some strange, wonderful way, shape, or form), it truly makes sense to first get centered, so the matters of the day flow out of a place far deeper than ourselves, CNN, or Facebook.

I'm sure some of you are really good at this already, and I commend you. For the rest of us, I wonder how it would change our days if we began each morning with just a minute or two or ten with God? I invite each of us to pause for just a bit – whether it is lying in bed after we've hit the snooze button, soaking up a hot shower, or sitting with that first cup of coffee. Within that pause, take a deep breath, give thanks for being alive, feel the joy and blessing of your moment of stillness, send love and light to those you are missing and concerned about, and just *be* for a few heartbeats.

I personally think these few moments could make the difference for the whole day. Start with stopping!

SILENCE

Benedictine monk, Brother David Steindl-Rast, has said, "Silence is the opportunity to let yourself down into mystery – to let yourself be touched by mystery. It is like the joy of music, only a thousand times deeper and greater."

Even though I am still isolating, I have two people (and a dog) in the house with me. Perhaps this is why I still appreciate silence. I imagine if I were alone, it might get tiring or even depressing. However, for now, when I can stop and appreciate it, silence feels like a warm, cozy blanket wrapped around me that can take me deep into myself and the Divine. Silence holds sacred space for all I am thinking and feeling, offering time and space to step back and truly see and hear what my unvarnished soul might have to express about the way things are. In this way, silence isn't emptiness or loneliness, but instead is a precious friend filled with awareness and insight. Eternal Silence sings my song back to me so that I might find my true self again and be free.

Silence is not something to fear, but something to seek out and to cherish. Today, may we all listen for what the Spirit of the Silence has to say to our hearts.

PARADISE AT HOME

Where is your happy place? Chances are, most of us would name a place quite far away. We're dreaming of beaches or mountains or fishing or the cabin (when there aren't repairs to do), etc. For me, it looks like a beach with sunshine, the rolling of the ocean, and a cabana boy to bring us fruity drinks while we play *Scrabble*. Sigh.

Thomas Merton once said, "Here is the unspeakable secret: paradise is all around us and we do not understand it." He is right. While I love my happy place, the truth is that, with an attitude adjustment, every place could be my happy place. Every place could be paradise.

When we return from a trip, most of us are usually overjoyed to be back in our own beds with our familiar stuff around us. I know we're probably all getting a little too much time with our own stuff these days, but with a slightly different angle, we can consider it time in the paradise that surrounds us.

Look with fresh eyes at the things in your life, those so familiar that you take them for granted. Our homes, our yards, the flowers poking their heads out of the soil, the squirrels and rabbits, the sunshine . . . paradise is right here. Paradise is not perfect. It is life. It has a snake and probably a runny nose now and again and gnats and bad breath. However, it can still take our breath away daily.

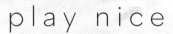

play nice

"We must remind ourselves that, though our
lives are small and our acts seem insignificant,
we are generative elements of this universe,
and we create meaning with each act that we
perform or fail to perform."
~ Kent Nerburn, *Make Me an Instrument
of Your Peace*

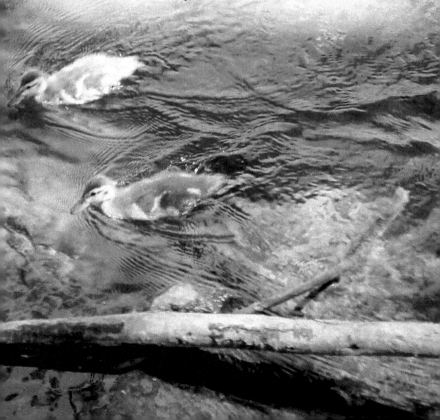

NACHO AND HIS WIFE

Unbeknownst to me, my twenty-four-year-old son, Sam (who lives in the Phoenix area), took one of his cars to a friend's friend in Mexico to have the upholstery redone. This seemed like a really bad idea to me, his mother, but no one asked me.

Anyway, getting the finished car back across the border wasn't nearly as easy. He drove down by himself, pulling a car trailer to tow the car home because the registration had expired. Border patrol wouldn't let him drive across, so he walked across and took a taxi to get his car. Long story short – he picked up the car, only to have it die in the middle of the road shortly thereafter. Thankfully, some kind soul pushed him out of the middle of the road, then another kind soul jumped his car, and Sam went to look for a battery store. The car died again not far from the store and two more kind souls, Nacho and his wife, pushed him out of the middle of the road again and then spent an hour and a half with him, helping him get a new battery and get back to the border. Getting the car back across the border was its own special kind of nightmare, but all Sam could say was, "Thank God for Nacho and his wife."

I find myself wondering if Nacho and his wife, or a young Black man, would have received the same kind of help in the U.S.? As a mother, it choked me up with gratitude to think someone helped my white, young, non-Spanish-speaking son in the middle of the blistering 110-degree heat in a Mexican border town. This is when the beauty of our souls becomes apparent. This is understanding our connectedness and thus treating others as we'd like to be treated. This is what the world needs so much more of.

It seems to me that the most sacred sound in the world comes from the heart and the soul. It doesn't require actual words, and it is called compassion. It is a deep sensing of someone's pain. It is letting someone else's tears fall down our cheeks. Compassion is a knowing and a trusting, but mainly, it is a doing. It is an act revealing our true nature – love.

A VISION OF PEACE

I have a few very distinct memories of my young children etched into my heart.

One happened when my daughter, Bryn, was five and we were at her older brother's basketball game. I brought some paper, coloring books, markers, and crayons to keep her busy. A few minutes after she started coloring, I felt a soft touch on my shoulder. It was a little African-American girl who was sitting on her daddy's lap. She didn't need to say anything. All she had to do was look at me with her beautiful brown eyes. I turned to Bryn and whispered in her ear, "How would you like to share your paper and crayons with the little girl behind us?" She glanced around me, then looked at me with a little smile and a nod.

About twenty minutes later, another African-American father and four kids sat down next to us. The little girl, who was about Bryn's age, and her younger brother just kept watching the girls coloring. Before long, Bryn asked me to invite them to also come color. Soon, all four were on the floor coloring. They were well-behaved, happy, and kind to one another. I was afraid Bryn wouldn't want to share her new markers with anyone, but she didn't mind sharing everything she had.

For a few brief, shining moments, there was a vision of what this world could be right before my eyes. It was the Kin-dom of God right there on the floor of a basketball court. It was how Jesus lived and called us to live – with peace, love, kindness, acceptance, generosity, and joy. I remember it, because such a vision is indeed unforgettable. I ache for this vision to be a reality.

LOVING IS NEVER JUDGING

Mother Teresa once said, "If you judge people, you have no time to love them."

She is *so* right. Jesus never said, "Judge others as I have judged you." Nope. He said, "*Love* others as I have loved you," (*John 13:34*). Heavy sigh. This is hard stuff.

For example, early on in the pandemic, I kept hearing people say, "Why are there still so many people on the roads?" I'd think to myself, "But *you're* out there, too!"

Or, here's one of my biggest struggles: I have an intolerance for intolerance. Especially religious intolerance, the whole "I'm right and you're wrong" thing. Letting a dogma or creed block the flow of your love or mercy drives me crazy.

"If you judge people, you have no time to love them."

Take a deep breath. Remember. If I approach people and situations with an attitude of judging, there is no room for loving them, as I am called to do. Sometimes it is really hard, almost impossible, not to let judging creep in. Okay, I fail on a fairly regular basis, but I keep trying, because each person has burdens they carry and their own hurts and fears that haunt them. I can never fully comprehend what motivates someone.

Loving another person doesn't mean I have to agree with them, bring them home and support them, or even become friends with them. It means I will do my best to see God in them (the spark of God *is* in every person) and to love the Essence of Light which shines within them . . . sometimes very deep within.

And then I pray that others will see past my own faults and failings as well. Simply claiming one's own very real and very many flaws is a surefire method of dousing the flames of judgement.

MENDING OUR
SELF-CENTERED WAYS

Play nice. Seems simple to me. Another way to put it is the Golden Rule: *Do unto others as you would have them do unto you.* Why, then, is this so hard?

Truth be told, I wasn't a very good big sister. My brother, Gary, is three years younger than me, and I'm afraid once he got old enough to follow me around, I didn't want much to do with him. The fact that he turned out to be a pretty great guy didn't have much to do with me. I put rocks in his diapers, unintentionally slammed his toe in a car door, was the (again, unintentional) cause of a few cases of stitches, rarely wanted to play games with him, and told him he couldn't hang with me and my friends. I'm not proud of this, but there you have it. I'm not entirely sure of the reason for my poor behavior, other than I was a fairly self-centered kid and I wanted what I wanted. I wanted to read books and play with my friends – alone.

I have grown up, mended my self-centered ways, and apologized multiple times (sorry again, Gary), but sometimes all of us get sucked back into a lower stage of growth where we don't consider others. Lately, it feels like our society is getting sucked back into that stage and doesn't give a hoot about what is best for the community or world as a whole.

Basically, I think it is all about awareness and practice. Yes, this means it may take some hard work on our part. We need to be aware of our knee-jerk reactions to others (judging them as stupid or annoying or bad), and instead choose to be nice, cooperative, and compassionate. Our reactions and behaviors are not someone else's fault. We take responsibility for what we say and what we do and whether we play nice or not. When we play nice, we allow the spark of the Divine to be witnessed and lived. When we are self-centered, ironically, this is the context for *losing* our center.

BE A BLESSING

Years ago, I read Jan Karon's wholesome novels about an Episcopal priest named Father Tim and the little town he served in. I honestly don't remember much about the books, except a prayer I learned. Each day when Father Tim went to the church to work, he would utter a prayer at the door, saying, "God make me a blessing to someone today." I have said this prayer many, many, many times since first reading it.

It reminds me that we should not seek so much to be blessed by God as to be a blessing to others.

For me, this short prayer opens up a deliberate invitation for the Spirit to move in me. Despite being isolated during these times, I believe it is still possible for us to be blessings to others. Follow your heart when it nudges you to make a phone call, write a note, send an email, drop off some flowers on someone's doorstep, leave encouraging messages in chalk on your sidewalk, or post a positive meme on Facebook. Be creative! All these little things make a big difference.

It invariably happens. When I am feeling most down about myself, about being a pastor, about my ability to reach people through my messages, it is then I receive a card or an email thanking me for something I've done or said. Those simple actions keep me going, and I always let them know what a blessing they were to me.

I invite you to try making this prayer part of your morning routine. Say it when you sip your first cup of coffee, when you are in the shower, or when you are waking up your computer for a day at your virtual office. Open yourself up to being God's instrument (from a safe distance, for now) in this world.

ABSURDITY OF MINISTRY

I took a class in seminary called "Empowerment." It was supposed to help us deepen our spirituality. On the first day of class, we were asked to give two words to describe our call to ministry. Well, I came up with three: *absurdity, skepticism, and faith*. Imagine how inadequate I felt when the others in the class were talking about passion, caretaking, discipleship, and all kinds of other wonderful, "religious-y" words. Nevertheless, I've revisited these words a few times over the years, and I still think they are accurate.

Becoming a pastor was absurd for many reasons, not the least of which was that I had *never* been on a church committee (blissfully ignorant), had never been in a Sunday School class (the only one I ever taught was for preschoolers, and the sanitized version of Noah's Ark was pretty easy), and I hadn't read much of the Bible, either – talk about clueless.

Then there was the absurdity of ditching any

sort of normal career for a vocation in institutional religion and dragging my family into something completely unknown. I should have had my head checked. Oh, wait, they did that before they gave me an appointment in a church.

If I really think about it, I guess I'm in good company. Jesus was pretty absurd himself. I mean, this guy had some awesome things to say and lived with a depth of compassion I'm not sure I can ever fully emulate – but he got himself killed! The disciples who shared his message after his death also risked their lives. Preaching about a resurrected dead guy fills the bill of absurdity, skepticism, and faith.

Plus, the world itself is pretty absurd – full of misplaced priorities, injustice, scary viruses, unnecessary suffering, inequity, and any number of things and opinions which simply make no reasonable (let alone common) sense.

Over time, I've come to realize how we are *all* called to minister (to be helpful, kind, and compassionate) in the midst of such absurdity. Jesus did. The disciples did. Millions of people have done so since then. It's just part and parcel of the whole spiritual gig.

in-between

"Being in liminal space is like swinging on
a trapeze. Once the handle is released there
is nothing to hold onto until the handle
on the other side is caught . . . Liminality
requires acceptance of mystery and a
heart full of trust. The challenge is to give
ourselves fully to the process of change
while being unsure and unclear of how this
liminal time will affect our future."

~ Joyce Rupp, *Open the Door*

FIVE STAGES OF
PANDEMIC GRIEF

I've decided that our progression through this pandemic is a good deal like the five stages of grief: *denial, anger, bargaining, depression, and acceptance.* Of course, as research has shown, this is not a linear process. One can jump back and forth between these stages for a long time.

Think about it. Our country *denied* it could ever get this bad here, many people denied that it was any different than the flu, some believed it wouldn't happen to them, and some believed the worst was over, so why wear a mask?

Anger came out with a vengeance when people screamed that their rights and freedoms were being taken from them, so they protested with weapons and hardly-veiled threats of anarchy.

Then there was the futile *bargaining.* Well, if I wear a mask, can I go to the store or get my hair cut or reopen my business? If we promise to stand far enough away, can we go to bars and restaurants and reopen the churches?

I've seen a lot of *depression* expressed as loneliness, lack of motivation, sadness, exhaustion, and a desire to eat copious amounts of ice cream. (Did anyone else notice the consistently empty shelves in the ice cream section?)

Occasionally, and perhaps with a little more frequency as time goes on, we have moments – maybe even hours or days – of *acceptance*. At these times, we admit this is where we are and will do our best to make the most of every day – in spite of the pandemic, not because of it.

So, what's my point? First, it helps to be aware of the different emotions we're feeling and to recognize that they are entrenched in this changing environment. We will probably go round and round with denial, anger, bargaining, depression, and acceptance more than once as the days creep by. Second, each one of us handles this bundle of conflicting emotions differently, so strive to be kind, understanding, and compassionate. Third, nobody wants this to be our new normal. Not me. Not you.

No one. However, this pandemic will evidently be with us for quite some time.

Finally, I believe acceptance and a sense of peace come as we let go more and more of what we want and embrace more and more of what we have. Truly, we still have each other, and life is still inherently good. This pandemic has forced us to stop, slow down, reflect, ponder, and pray. It is up to us whether we make this time a spiritually productive one or not.

Our souls are indeed being stretched.

A PLACE TO CRY

There is a palpable sense of grief to these pandemic days. We grieve the now seemingly easy days of moving about the world with very little worry of getting sick. We grieve the simple act of going out to eat with friends. We grieve the lost time with grandchildren and children. We grieve all our kids have lost in school, time with friends, sports and theater, and all the fun things one can only do in person. Not to mention the grief we feel over the death of millions of people around the world.

There is also a palpable sense of grief for the racial situation in this country. We grieve something we've never had: a world where color doesn't matter. We grieve the trust that was never there to lose. We grieve the fear that accompanies parenting a child of color. We grieve the friendships we could have if only the world were different. We grieve the trauma that people of color have suffered for centuries and continue to suffer.

Clarence Forsberg tells a story of visiting a little chapel out in the Pacific Northwest, which had stained glass windows and a beautiful altar. As he left the church, he stopped to sign the guest registry. Leafing through the pages to see if he recognized any of the names, he spied one particular entry. No name was listed, just the date and these words, "Thank you for a place to cry."

Some days, our souls simply need a safe place to cry. Who provides you with a trustworthy place to shed your tears? Even Jesus wept. This, too, is sacred.

ACTIVE WAITING

I looked at my dog one morning and said, "Is this what it's like being a dog? Same thing every day?" She didn't answer, but she did look at me knowingly with her sweet, brown eyes. She gets it. Yet she seems okay with it. Sure, she gets excited when we're going for a walk, but she spends most of her day patiently relaxing, napping, and watching the animals and birds out the window. We have much to learn from our pets.

I know, I know, it just isn't that easy. They don't have to pay the bills, make dinner, mow the lawn, do laundry, and take care of their kids, or grandkids, or parents. Even so, we could learn a lesson or two about waiting patiently and waiting in a way that fills us up spiritually.

I know many of us are working, and some of us have tried to resume some "normal" activities, but we're still playing the waiting game with this virus. The truth is that most of us aren't very good at waiting, and our culture has conditioned us to believe that waiting is bad and doing nothing is lazy.

So, perhaps we need to rethink the concept of waiting. I believe there is such a thing as active waiting, which can be beneficial for our souls. Active waiting means we aren't getting caught up in the worry and anxiety or in the boredom and drudgery, but instead we're using our time productively and wisely. It means we are finding ways to fill our days with things that are meaningful for us. It means that we're not ignoring our feelings, our souls, our struggles, or our spirituality. It means that when we look back at this time, we'll be able to see how all that waiting truly helped us grow.

Evelyn Underhill said, "A lot of the road to heaven has to be taken at thirty miles an hour." Life is just like that . . . We have to take a lot of it at thirty miles an hour. Sure, we'd love to speed through some of the boring parts or the difficult parts, but it's not designed that way.

PUZZLE PIECES

I think 2020 at our house will be known as *The Year of the Puzzles*. We finished more puzzles (most were 1,000 pieces) in 2020 than I may have done in my entire life! It kept us out of trouble (somewhat) and was something we could do together in the evenings or when we needed a little break during the day. We especially love puzzles that come with a larger poster-type picture of what the puzzle looks like, so it is easier for aging eyes to spot where those weird-looking pieces actually go.

Rachel Remen, in her book *Kitchen Table Wisdom*, talks about the puzzle table her father gave to her mother as a birthday present one year. All through her childhood, her parents kept a puzzle going on that table, but her father always hid the box top! I suggested this to my partner once, but her response wasn't exactly fit for public consumption.

Truly, life seems to be more like putting together

the pieces of a puzzle without having a nice, big picture to follow! We take life one piece at a time, the bright, colorful ones and the darker, gloomier ones and the ones that don't look like they go to our puzzle at all, and we do our best to fit it into the whole of our lives. It's usually not until much later that we see the picture the pieces make as a whole. It's only then that we can truly appreciate the importance and profound meaning of each piece.

What we're going through now will be more pieces in our puzzles. And someday, with the benefit of hindsight, we'll see how this has helped shape us and the world as we know it. One piece at a time.

TREASURE IN THE
WILDERNESS

In the Bible, there is a story of Jesus spending forty days in the wilderness before beginning his ministry. Clearly it was a transformative time for him where he grew in wisdom and confidence in himself and God. I wonder if, at the end of all this, we'll be able to say the same.

Just because the wilderness experience was transformative for Jesus doesn't mean it was easy. They rarely are. In the wilderness, we're bound to come across all sorts of things we don't like . . . wild beasts, bad weather, heavy burdens, baggage, hunger, loneliness, fear, longing, and darkness. But if one has courage and resilience, the wilderness also holds enormous treasures more valuable than gold, silver, or a year's supply of toilet paper!

"What treasure is this?" you ask. It is the treasure of wisdom, the kind that is only born through struggle

(which is really annoying, but there you have it). It is the treasure of deeper understanding of ourselves and the world. And, it is the treasure of becoming more authentic.

Here are a few critical things to keep in mind in the wilderness. First, you've survived the wilderness before, and you will again. Yes, this too shall pass – trite, but true. Second, take deep breaths. When we get anxious or scared, we breathe shallowly. A deep breath slows us, grounds us, gives us a chance to regain perspective so we can cultivate much desired wisdom. Third, we are never alone, even when we *feel* alone. Not only is the Eternal Essence with us, but everyone who has ever been, is, or will be is also with us.

LIMINAL SPACE

Is it just me, or is there something about the "days after" which makes us melancholy and reluctant to go back to life as usual? I think about the day after a wedding, Christmas, a birthday party, a vacation, or any fun gathering or celebration. As odd as it sounds, I'd even include deathbed vigils and funerals of close loved ones in this category.

Perhaps it is because on these "days after," we participate in a few moments or hours of sacred space, or *liminal* space – an in-between place where the ordinary and the Something More seem much closer than usual.

Liminal space has the effect that a potter has on clay. We are molded and shaped, albeit slowly, and we're apt to go back into the world and smash whatever shaping was done. Still, liminal space gives us a new perspective and reminds us of what is truly important in life. Liminal space reminds us we are not alone, we are loved, the core of our being is light and love . . . and so is everyone else's. We've just forgotten or been too busy to take note.

The key to the liminal experience is that it helps create us anew. I know it is slow. I know we don't necessarily trust it once we're back in the "real" world, as it feels too faraway and maybe too magical to be true. However, what if it is *more* real and *truer* than what we perceive to be true in our everyday lives?

Be changed. Be made more whole. Be more loving, forgiving, and compassionate (to yourself as well as others). Be more joyful, hopeful, and peaceful. Be who you were created to be . . . the beautiful, unique you.

THE GAP

One of the most uncomfortable places to be is in the gap – a space between what was and what is yet to come. It reminds me of the experience of going between the countries of Jordan and Israel on a bus. We went through security on one side, then the bus drove through a section of land with walls so high we couldn't see our surroundings, until we got to the other side where we went through security again. In that short distance, we were neither here nor there. What we'd left was gone, but what was coming couldn't yet be seen.

This gap was short-lived. I've stood in the gap for much longer (metaphorically speaking) and have basically found it to be not only uncomfortable, but also scary and lonely all at the same time. It would be easy to get caught up worrying about the gap, worrying about when I/we will get through it, worrying about what things will look like on the other side. But . . . we all know how worrying doesn't change anything. So, I work on taking a deep breath and living in each moment with as much kindness, patience, and compassion as I can.

Gaps can be like tunnels. Eerie. Dark. A bit frightening. However, every tunnel has an end. There will always be gaps to live through; the only question is *how* will we live through them?

hope

———————

"When you don't know what to
preach . . . preach hope."
~ Dr. Henry Young

LESSONS FROM TINY WINGS

We are fortunate enough to see a few hummingbirds zooming around our flowers every year. I finally decided to buy a feeder for them and hang it just off the back deck so we could see them better. Of course, they prefer the flowers.

Just for fun, I decided to do a little research on the hummingbirds. Did you know that, according to *Hummingbird Central*, they migrate to Central America or Mexico every year? And that they travel alone, flying up to twenty-three miles per day with their hearts beating up to 1,260 times a minute and their wings flapping fifteen to eighty times per second? They are such delicate, little creatures to make such a huge trek and expend so much energy. I simply shake my head in impressed amazement.

I got to thinking how perhaps they're an example for us in these challenging times. I imagine they don't really know how far they are traveling but simply know when they get there. Clearly, they have an inner guidance system they rely upon for their path, and while their journey is solitary, that doesn't seem to bother them. It's just the way it is.

In these days of COVID-19, we're all on a long, long journey without a road map. We don't know how things are going to play out or how long this is going to last, but we'll know the end when we see it! To survive this time well, it helps to rely on something we also can't see – our Inner Wisdom, Divine Guidance, Universal Consciousness, Higher Self, God, Goddess, Spirit, Love Energy. It has a multitude of names and images, but the One is always present to strengthen, comfort, calm, guide, and support us in the journey.

These spiritual journeys of ours are inherently solitary. We may walk with others, learn from others, and care for and support others along the way, but the transformation which can happen on this crazy journey, well, it happens way down deep inside.

Those little hummingbirds give me strength, hope, and courage for the journey. Certainly, if they can fly thousands of miles alone, we too can drum up the courage to keep moving forward one step at a time, not knowing what each new day will bring but trusting in the invisible wings of the Spirit to bear us up.

IN LOVE WITH A VISION

Shirley Chisholm was the first Black woman elected to the United States Congress in 1968. In 1972, she sought the presidential nomination from the Democratic Party. When she was asked why she – a Black woman – was running for president, she responded, "Because I am in love with the America that does not yet exist."

Why did Jesus try so hard to reform Judaism? Why did Mother Teresa try so hard to care for the poor and dying in Calcutta? Why did Millard Fuller leave a promising career to start Habitat for Humanity? Why does anyone volunteer for a nonprofit organization? Why does anyone raise money for a cause? Why go on a mission trip? Why do we write to our senators and representatives? Why do we march for social justice? Why? Even when it seems like we don't have a chance, why?

Because we are in love with a vision that doesn't yet exist. This is hope.

The true leaders today, in my humble opinion, are acknowledging the brokenness of our justice system and the insidious shadow of racism which permeates our world. At the very same time, these leaders are calling us to hope. This crisis, as awful as it is, may be the catalyst we need to begin to make real, lasting change. They are calling us to a vision which doesn't yet exist and telling us we are *all* part of making this vision happen.

Through our actions – big and small – we each contribute to creating the world we live in. Whether you teach children, heal people, defend our country, bring food to a sick friend, hold the door open for a stranger, serve food to the homeless, donate to the food pantry, make a blanket for refugee children, or pray for our leaders . . . when you take action for a vision you love, you bring hope.

Part of being a hope-bearer in this moment in time means we need to examine our own hearts and minds, and we need to purge our own judgements and prejudices from our souls. (We have them, whether we want to believe it or not.) We need to confront racism and misinformation when we find it. We need to get off the sidelines and stand up again and again, this time standing on the side of love.

IT COULD BE WORSE

This time of quarantining or staying at home puts a whole new perspective on Anne Frank and her family, who spent 761 days in hiding during the Nazi occupation of Amsterdam during World War II. 761 days! Can you imagine? No sunshine on your face (except maybe through a window), no fresh air, no loud noise, no new people, no shopping, no work for over two years. Here we are complaining about a few months of self-isolating, even though we can still do most of the things they couldn't risk.

With everything going on around them and the stress of danger upon them every day, it certainly could not have been easy. Anne wondered why the adults slept and bickered so much. I imagine depression, fear, anger, uncertainty, sadness, loneliness, and boredom had a good deal to do with it.

Still, Anne wrote many things which showed how she retained a sense of hope and courage through it all. Despite everything, she believed in the basic goodness of people, actively looked for beauty, and let it lift her up. She held on to her ideals and sense of humor, and she knew full well that kindness and a gentle spirit were her strongest allies.

Anne wrote, "I feel the suffering of millions, but when I look up at the sky, I somehow feel that this cruelty too shall end and peace and tranquility will return once more."

We know there is suffering around the world today, but may these small moments of hope give us courage and strength to keep living with generosity, compassion, kindness, and gentleness. Optimism is never naïve. Optimism is clinging to what we know makes life and ourselves better.

CHALK DRAWINGS

Early on in the pandemic, I was tickled by the fact that four houses in the neighborhood had friendly, encouraging chalk messages at the ends of their driveways. One said, "Hi Neighbor! Enjoy your day!" Another said, "Be of good cheer! Wash your hands!" And a third said, "Stay well neighbor!" Plus, there were hearts, rainbows, and flowers – it was awesome and healing.

It's interesting how forced isolation compelled many people to reach out in ways they never did before. There is much we couldn't do under lockdown, but as Mother Teresa said, "We can do small things with great love."

If a chalk message from a child can make me smile and feel cared for by a neighbor I hardly know and have never spoken to, imagine the many small things we can do to give people a little pick-me-up. Perhaps this shared suffering will help us remember that we are all connected. Even though we have a six-foot social distancing space between us, perhaps we'll learn to break down the other barriers which have plagued our world (pun intended) in recent years. This crisis has the potential to unite us in ways other things have not – at least, that is my hope.

I'll tell you this. It wasn't long before I was outside with my colored chalk, writing messages to my neighbors at the end of my driveway! Hope is contagious.

HOPE IS ...

Sometimes it helps to just pause and remember all the things that bring us hope.

Hope is ...

... the music of the soul.

... fragile as the petals on a new flower in spring, yet strong enough to have pushed through hard soil.

... a soft rain on parched ground.

... a robin on a cloudy, damp, dreary day.

... a sunrise breaking through the night sky.

... a warm whisper of wind against our faces after a long, cold winter.

... a new pack of markers, a fresh box of crayons, a blank journal.

... packets of seeds waiting to be planted.

... a friend you can count on.

... the cry of a baby.

... a new sketchbook, a fresh skein of yarn, a few yards of fabric.

. . . a hot cup of tea (or whatever you love best), a soft blanket, a good book or recording.

. . . puppy kisses when you're down.

. . . a kind word, a helping hand, a note of encouragement.

. . . a candle in the dark . . .

I could go on, and I imagine you could easily add to the list. Even in the darkest of hours, on the bleakest days, hope surrounds us if we just look. For me, there is no greater evidence the Spirit is alive and well and on the move. When we act with hope, we align with the Essence of All That Is in a daring act of courage that says, "Bring it on. We will not cave, we will not crumble. We will hold each other up. We will go on in love, not despair."

Be hope today.

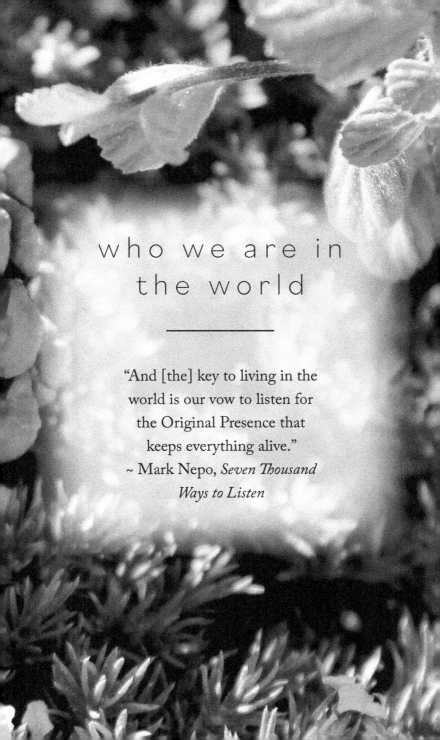

who we are in the world

―――――――

"And [the] key to living in the
world is our vow to listen for
the Original Presence that
keeps everything alive."
~ Mark Nepo, *Seven Thousand
Ways to Listen*

NO STRINGS ATTACHED

Because our mission trips to the Appalachia region always took place over two days, we would stop at a park or somewhere on Sunday morning for a brief worship service. One of our favorite places to worship was on the top of a cliff overlooking a natural bridge rock formation at Natural Bridge State Park in Kentucky.

One year, I asked the group to pick up a rock on their way up the mountain and bring it to worship. When we had gathered, I began by telling them a Dorothy Day story as told by author Parker Palmer in his book, *Let Your Life Speak*. He wrote:

"Years ago, I heard Dorothy Day speak. Founder of the Catholic Worker movement, her long-term commitment to living among the poor on New York's Lower East Side - not just serving them but sharing their condition - had made her one of my heroes. So it came as a great shock when in the middle of her talk, I heard her start to ruminate about the "ungrateful poor." I did not understand how such a dismissive phrase could come from the lips of a saint - until it hit me with the force of a Zen koan. Dorothy Day was saying, 'Do not give to the poor expecting to get their gratitude so that you can feel good about yourself. If you do, your giving will be thin and short-lived, and that is not what the poor need; it will only impoverish them further. Give only if you have something you must give; give only if you are someone for whom giving is its own reward.'"

It's hard, sometimes, not to expect to be thanked or rewarded when we've helped someone else. We want to be appreciated to boost our own self-esteem and give our egos a lift. We want to have someone pat us on the back and tell us how awesome we are. But pure service is meant to be given without attachments and expectations.

After the story, I invited our group to let their rocks symbolize something that they were bringing as their gift to the people of Appalachia that week and to place them on our huge makeshift stone altar. I was pleasantly surprised and impressed when these gifts were clearly well thought-out. People brought compassion, kindness, a desire for understanding, acceptance, hope, non-judgement, patience, and so much more.

The world needs such gifts from us, given without strings, given simply because it is what we do, because it is who we are.

SAVE THE TURTLES

One of the odd adages of the Appalachia Service Project (ASP) is: *thou must save the turtles!* You see, there are wonderful, big, old box turtles and snapping turtles who wander their way out onto the highways of Appalachia and are liable to be crushed under the wheels of a truck unless some kind soul stops to help them across. Single-minded creatures that they are, you must always move them in the direction they are heading, or they'll simply turn around and head back out onto the road.

Over the years, many, many, many turtles have been saved by ASP crews. But there is a deeper lesson here to be gleaned.

On ASP (or in life, for that matter), it's easy to become as single-minded as that turtle. We figure we have a job that we've come down here to do and, by golly, we intend to get it done, come hell or high water (both of which I've seen in Appalachia). In this state of mind, it's easy to rush back and forth from the center we stay at to our work site without paying much attention in between. Watching for turtles requires thinking about something other than ourselves and our project for a little bit.

It feels to me like this could be a good spiritual motto for life on a daily basis: slow down, be aware of your surroundings, and take care of the turtles crossing your path.

A word of caution, however. If you happen to run across a snapping turtle, use a shovel!

PROBLEM OR INCONVENIENCE?

Robert Fulghum, in the book, *Stories to Live By*, tells a great story about when he was twenty-two and working as a night clerk at a lodge in the Sierra Nevada Mountains of Northern California. One week, the staff had been served the exact same thing for lunch every day: hot dogs and sauerkraut. To top it off, the cost of the meal was deducted from their meager paychecks.

Well, Friday night rolled around, and Robert went into the kitchen to get a bite to eat when he discovered a note to the chef saying that hot dogs and sauerkraut would be on the employee menu for two more days. Lacking much of an audience at eleven p.m., Robert found Sigmund Wollman, the night auditor, and went into a twenty-minute rant. He'd had it, he was quitting, he was going to throw a plate of hot dogs and sauerkraut at the owner! This was un-American, the resort sucked, and the guests were all idiots, etc. etc. Plus, it was punctuated by the kicking of chairs, pounding of tables, and much profanity.

Sigmund (a survivor of Auschwitz, by the way, so think German accent when you read this) sat quietly through it all, smoking a cigarette. When Robert wound down, Sigmund said, *"Fulchum, you think you know everything, but you don't know the difference between an inconvenience and a problem. If you break your neck, if you have nothing to eat, if your house is on fire--then you got a problem. Everything else is inconvenience. Life is inconvenient. Life is lumpy. Learn to separate the inconveniences from the real problems. You will live longer. And will not annoy people like me so much. Good night."*

This seems like good advice during this crazy pandemic. Not being able to eat in a restaurant, not going in public without a mask, not going to church or the movies or the State Fair or a concert or a sporting event . . . these are all inconveniences. Keeping our center means learning to get some perspective and not letting our energy and joy get sucked up by inconveniences.

When stressed out, frustrated, or angry, perhaps it's time to ask ourselves, "Problem or inconvenience?"

SHOW ME YOUR FAITH

Every once and a while I just need to say this . . .

I'm tired of the loudest Christian voices spouting hatred and claiming it comes from God.

I'm tired of people who quote Bible verses as if this is what it means to be faithful.

I'm tired of people spouting their beliefs as if everyone needs the right answer to join the club.

I'm tired of fear-based, guilt-inducing, shame-ridden religion.

I'm tired of televangelists saying, "Show me the money!" when people want to be blessed.

I'm tired of people co-opting the name Christian to advance their own selfish, narrow-minded goals.

Don't scream your beliefs at me, *show me how your faith changes the way you live.*

Show me that you actually listen to the stories of Jesus when he tells us to love our neighbor as ourselves, love our enemies, and turn the other cheek.

Show me your faith by listening to and respecting people who are different.

Show me your faith by wearing a mask to protect your health and the health of others.

Show me your faith by living compassionately.

Show me your faith by trying to understand and not judge.

Show me your faith by speaking kind, encouraging words and kicking to the curb the little gremlin inside you that wants to be negative and critical.

Show me your faith by voting for those who care more about people than corporations and money.

Show me your faith by standing with and for the oppressed.

Show me your faith by erring on the side of love over and over and over again.

If your faith in Something More is not changing the way you think and live so that more light, love, justice, and harmony are created in the world, then your faith is simply empty words.

Just sayin' . . .

VULNERABILITY

Over the many weeks I was writing reflections, I found I received the most feedback about the ones in which I shared a personal story or my feelings and allowed myself to be vulnerable. It doesn't mean I was being weak. It means I was consciously risking showing you part of myself in hopes that you wouldn't smash my ego to bits, and that you would be able to relate and we would connect on a spiritual level.

Spirituality is relational. It doesn't exist in a vacuum. It exists because of a connection between us and the Essence of All That Is, whether this is a mystical connection, or a connection with another person, your dog or cat, nature, music, poetry, art, or whatever.

The pastor I finished my student pastoring with was excellent and a really good preacher, but she hardly ever shared anything about herself in a sermon. Not that everything should be about the person preaching, but an occasional anecdote is nice. Anyway, she rarely allowed herself to be vulnerable – I get it. Still, at the time, I knew there was a key element of connection which was missing because she was afraid to let anyone past the wall she had erected.

As Brené Brown states in her book, *Daring Greatly*, "Vulnerability is the core, the heart, the center, of meaningful human experiences." Perhaps this is what we've lost in our modern, achieving, consuming, independent, dog-eat-dog world. We risk our true selves much less, we don't like to ask for help, we shut down or shut out when we're hurt, we don't typically ask others about their stories, and no one asks us for ours. We wonder if anyone truly cares.

I'm not saying we need to let it all hang out on Facebook. Seriously, there is such a thing as oversharing. We need to be judicious about who we share with, and why. However, if we're going to make honest progress in this world around racism, sexism, homophobia, ageism, and so much more, we have to risk sharing our stories and feelings, and we have to risk really listening to others.

The tie which truly binds us together is our human vulnerability.

THE MOVIE OF OUR LIVES

Sometimes we get so caught up in our lives that we lose perspective. What if we took a step back and looked at our lives as if they were movies playing out in front of us? They could be love stories, dramas, comedies, tragedies, or adventures, depending on the day – hopefully no horror.

Consider that we are not just actors in these movies of our lives, but we are also the writers, audiences, critics, and fans. Unlike puppets controlled by an unseen hand, we have control over our lines and actions, even if we don't have control over others.

From the perspective of the audience, what do you see? Do you want to applaud or cringe? Are you making good decisions? Are you treating people with kindness? Are you seeking understanding? Are you standing up for what you believe in? Or are you forcing your agenda? Are you snapping at people around you? Are you stuck in a rut of your own making? You get my drift . . . What do you *really* see on the big screen of your life?

Now, from the perspective of the script writer, how will you move forward? What kind of person would you like to see yourself become? You have choices to make. You can continue the way you were or perhaps find things you'd like to change. You still have a limited budget and no money to hire different actors. You'll have to make do with the set as it is, but you have complete control over your words and movements. What will today look like?

Remember, a good movie always has a good ending. Wrap up each day with a positive attitude and perspective. Find a tiny miracle within every day. Make it count.

HUMAN *BEINGS*

I wonder all kinds of weird things. Like, I wonder if we all should shed the notion of ourselves as nouns, things, objects. We are human *beings* after all.

English anthropologist, Gregory Bateson, was fond of saying, "Stamp out all nouns." His theory was basically that once you've given something a name, you have created a label that can then be categorized, judged, stereotyped, and separated from all else. I don't personally know how you get rid of nouns and still communicate, but I appreciate the sentiment.

As Ulysses S. Grant was dying of throat cancer in 1885, he said, "The fact is, I think I am a verb instead of a personal pronoun. A verb is anything that signifies to be; to do; or to suffer. I signify all three."

Let us see ourselves as generative, creative movements upon the earth. With our very essence, we are called to be bearers of light, beacons of hope, arms of compassion, and words of peace. This is the core of our *being*. This is what it means to *be yourself*. The pettiness, the anger toward the way people behave or believe, the fear of not being enough, the self-criticism or loathing, our sharp tongues and passive-aggressive jabs are *not* part of our deepest, truest *being*.

Be awake. Be aware. Be present. Be grace. Be Sabbath for others. Be genuine. Be rigorously honest. Be open to all of life, each and every bittersweet morsel of it.

THE LEAST WE CAN DO

I don't know why our house gets so dusty, but it does. And it is really hard to find motivation to clean when no one can come over anyway. Still, I have some standards and was running a cloth over some of the surfaces last week when my partner looked at me and said, "Oh, you're cheater-dusting." Yep. Deal with it. I wasn't in the mood to take everything off every surface. And if there is a runner on the table, it isn't dusty *under* the runner anyway, right? It was the least I could do.

I think we use that phrase fairly often, "Well, it's the least I can do." How come we don't do the *best* we can do? Why do we send a card instead of going to the funeral? Why do we determine how little we can get away with spending for a wedding or birthday? What's the least I can give to that charity and still get an umbrella? What's the least I need to get on that final to get an A in the class? What's the least I can do and still call myself spiritual or religious? I've seen wall plates and outlet plates painted over instead of people taking the time to remove them before repainting a room. Oh, the list could go on and on.

Is it sheer laziness? Lack of time? Lack of caring? It seems to me that we should strive to do our best in all things, especially when it comes to showing our love and care for other people, as well as ourselves.

I don't claim to be perfect, and obviously my dusting integrity needs work. But this concept is in my consciousness now, which means I actually have to think about it. And it's in yours now, too! How will we act in the future? Will we do the least we can do, or the best?

KEEP THE FAITH

The opposite of faith is not doubt; it is certainty. Heaven knows I didn't have any certainty when I entered seminary. I had a very pure, simple faith that there was Something More. It wasn't anything factual or anything I could prove. It wasn't because "the Bible told me so." I just knew. I still do.

The truth of the matter is that I don't have any more certainty now than I did then; it just bothers me less. I really, really, *really* wanted solid answers to my questions in seminary. Gratefully, I was in a place where they didn't give them to me. Instead, I was encouraged to ask more and more questions, to listen to my heart, and to measure truth based on love, kindness, and justice.

In *The Gifts of Imperfection*, Brené Brown defines faith as *"a place of mystery, where we find the courage to believe in what we cannot see and the strength to let go of our fear of uncertainty."* As it always seems to be with the spiritual path, this is easier said than done. Yet, if we have faith that we are one with the One Who Is Love, surely some of this fear should ease.

One of my favorite movie lines of all times is from the *Sound of Music* when Mother Superior says to Sister Berthe, *"I always try to keep faith in my doubts."* No matter how challenging or scary life gets, this is my goal.

A GRATEFUL SKEPTIC

"There lives more faith in honest doubt,
believe me, than in half the creeds."
~ Alfred Lord Tennysen

I've always made a great Doubting Thomas or Devil's Advocate, because I'm skeptical (and even cynical) about so much related to church and religion. I'm not saying this is a good thing; it just is what it is. I think it's inherited from my father, who was an atheist when I was growing up – you know, the kind of atheist who invites the Jehovah's Witnesses in to argue about the existence of God. (He's no longer an atheist, but that's another story.)

The good thing about being skeptical about God and religion is that I find myself asking lots of questions and continually searching for answers. There is a concept in theology called the "hermeneutics of suspicion." This essentially means that when interpreting a text, one must look deeper than face value, challenge the cultural assumptions we make, question what might be going on, and seek to determine whether it happened at all or if it is a story told for a purpose. You get the gist. I love this sort of thing! (Weirdo . . . I know . . . I have no idea why I like this stuff.)

Anyway, the week after Easter, we always hear the story of the disciple Thomas who refused to believe Jesus had risen until he could "put his finger in the nail marks and hand into the spear wound" (*John 20:25*). As the story goes, Jesus met him right where he was in his skepticism and, without judgment, offered Thomas the opportunity to touch him. It was this graceful action which enabled Thomas to move forward, exclaiming, "My Savior and my God!"

We're not turned away because of our skepticism. To the contrary, it is through our skepticism the Divine finds ways to help us to grow. There is nothing wrong with being skeptical, as long as we hang in there and keep engaging this crazy, exciting, wonderfully absurd spiritual journey.

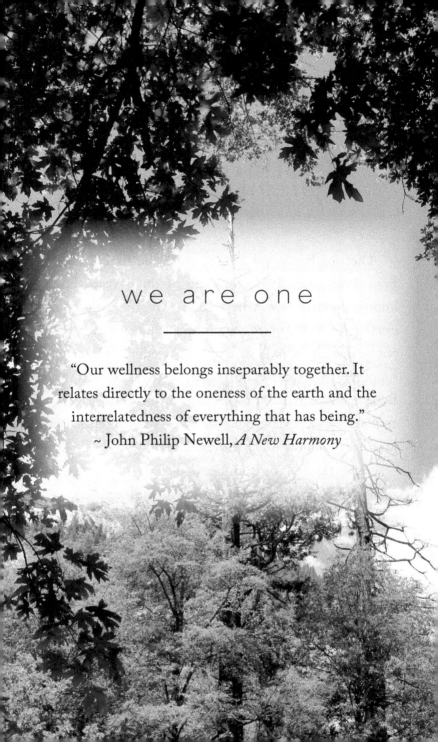

we are one

"Our wellness belongs inseparably together. It relates directly to the oneness of the earth and the interrelatedness of everything that has being."
~ John Philip Newell, *A New Harmony*

SOLIDARITY IN
DISAGREEMENT

Dictator Ferdinand Marcos ruled the Philippines from 1965 until 1986; for nine of those years, he imposed martial law. After winning again in a rigged election in 1986, massive numbers of people turned out to march in protest. Even the Catholic Church supported the protests. However, when some of the Benedictine nuns took to the streets, there was some conflict in the convent about whether it was appropriate for nuns to protest, much less risk arrest.

As Kathleen Norris, in her book *Dakota*, told the story: *"In a group meeting that began and ended with prayer, the sisters who wished to continue demonstrating explained that this was for them a religious obligation; those who disapproved also had their say. Everyone spoke; everyone was heard and gave counsel. It was eventually decided that the nuns who were demonstrating should continue to do so; those who wished to express solidarity but were unable to march would prepare food and provide medical assistance to the demonstrators, and those who disapproved would pray for everyone. The sister laughed and said, 'If one of the conservative sisters was praying that we young, crazy ones would come to our senses and stay off the streets, that was O.K. We were still a community.'"*

I will march today in a rally here in Racine put on by the Racine Coalition for Peace and Justice. I do so fully aware of the health risks, even though masks will be mandatory. I personally feel that I cannot continue to sit on the sidelines at this particular juncture in history, though I completely respect everyone's personal decision in this area. I want to go and stand with my Black brothers and sisters for justice and equality. Change never happens unless allies and supporters step up for the minority, and I am actively hoping and praying that all this brings positive change.

The story from the Philippines is a powerful example of listening and mutual respect. If only all conflicts could be met with such care. In social media, in the news, and in encounters others have shared, I know there is much disdain, if not concern, being expressed about the protests taking place. I know many of you probably have concerns about my involvement. Please know that I will take as much care as possible to remain safe. If you are able to join me, please do. If you are unable to walk, or disagree, please pray. We are a community. We are one.

COMMUNITY

Did we really know how important community was before we were forced to self-isolate? Before this virus, did we think about what it would mean to be suddenly separated from our church communities, our card clubs, our book groups, our walking groups, or support groups... not to mention our families, friends, and neighbors? Truthfully, we probably took them all for granted, at least to some extent.

Mark Nepo, in his book *The Exquisite Risk*, tells a story about an apprentice and a master:

"No matter who the apprentice talked to, if she listened close enough and long enough, the words all went back to the same source, as if there were only one large thing speaking. No matter how many eyes she looked deeply into, they all eventually revealed the same shimmer, as if there were only one large thing seeing. No matter how many pains she soothed, the cries all

sounded from the same human hurt, as if there were only one large thing feeling.

When she brought all this to her master, her master walked her in silence through the woods to a clearing where they sat on a fallen tree. The light was flooding through, covering everything. The master placed a stone in her one hand and a small flower in the other, and said, "Feel their warmth. See how both are covered differently with the same light. Now trace the light of each back to the sun."

The apprentice heard the one large thing speaking in the master's voice, saw the one large thing shimmer in the master's eyes, and even felt the same human hurt in the master's soft silence. The light grew even stronger and the master said, "We are all just small stones and little flowers yearning for the sun. What you have seen under words, behind many eyes, and beneath all cries is the One Direction."

I think the hidden superpower of any *healthy* community is that we begin to see under each other's words, behind each other's eyes, and within each other's cries – One Essence of All. The superpower of community reminds us we are not alone, but rather part of something much bigger, stronger, fuller – *whole*.

When, where, and how do you experience community? Without it, our lives run the risk of becoming very small, closing us in, enabling our fears and worries to run rampant. Communities challenge us to become bigger than we are, they embrace us in our pain, they hold us accountable for our actions, and perhaps most importantly, they give us a place to belong so that we do not feel so alone in this vast, mysterious universe.

HUGS NEEDED

Hugs. I think it's hugs I miss the most.

I know I am luckier than many folks, as I have people in my home to hug. Okay, I confess, I hugged my dad, too . . . just once . . . but I was masked, turned my head, and held my breath. It didn't seem the same.

When I was a pastor in the United Methodist Church, we were basically taught not to hug. I suppose they thought pastors should maintain an appropriate social and emotional distance from their parishioners. I didn't like that rule, although I always asked permission to hug if I was unsure how someone felt about it.

I'll never forget the one Sunday morning that I was greeting people after worship, and one of the elderly women in the congregation gave me a hug and said, "You're the only hug I get all week." I don't know why she and her husband weren't hugging each other anymore, but I felt sad I was it. She's part of the reason I wouldn't give it up.

I have often told folks that you should have at least ten hugs a day. Apparently, I was slightly wrong. In a *Healthline* article entitled "The Benefits of Hugging" family psychotherapist Virginia Satir asserts, "We need 4 hugs a day to survive, 8 hugs to be maintain ourselves and 12 hugs to grow."

Scientifically, it has been proven that hugging lowers one's heart rate and blood pressure, slows down breathing, relieves tension and agitation, and helps us develop a state of calm and well-being. Hugging increases the level of oxytocin, which allows us to connect better with others. And hugging significantly reduces the level of cortisol (the stress hormone) in the blood.

In another article on *Psychology Spot* entitled "How many hugs a day do we need to be happy?" researchers say that hugging helps us to have a better self-body-image. They have even gone so far as to say that "a lack of hugging or caressing could be a trigger − or an aggravation − for body image disorders like anorexia and bulimia."

Psychologist Jennifer Delago relates, "[Hugs]

even had a protective effect. When people received a hug, they had less conflict the next day and the bad mood for everyday problems was minor."

During WWII, the Nazi hospitals and orphanages often lacked sufficient staff. They conducted an awful study of newborns in which half received physical affection and attention, while the other half did not – every baby in the latter half died within weeks or months.

Given all of this, it's really crappy that hugging is sort of taboo because of this darn virus. Someday, will we have a new statistic of people who suffered or died from hug deprivation?

This sounds weird, I know, but we can all self-hug. Yes, it's a thing. I tried it, and it's kind of nice. Just cross your arms over your chest or stomach and give yourself the kind of hug you need – strong and bracing, or gentle and soothing. You can even add a little rocking to it if you feel like it. Too weird for you? Try stroking your arms in a sort of self-massage. This feels nice, too!

But if you are with people you can hug, then *do it*! Often!

FREEDOM

Annoyingly, the concept of freedom seems to have been hijacked by those who don't want to wear a mask. The much greater issue is how many people in this country are still not free to simply be who they are, wherever they are.

My partner reminded me of this simple fact when we were planning a mini-vacation for some hiking and kayaking. We rented a house in a small town up north, and we were looking at the facts about the town when she said, "I'm not sure we should be holding hands in public there." Now, maybe she was seeing red flags where there weren't any, but the fact we even have to *think* about it means we're not free here – yet.

Until a Black person can walk safely down any street, dressed however they wish, we are not free. Until a trans person can stand on a street corner without being afraid of becoming a victim of a hate crime, we are not free. Until immigrant children are not kept in cages, we are not free. Until youth who are different are not bullied, we are not free. Until women are paid the same as men and are no longer seen as sexual objects, we are not free. I'm sure you could add more.

Freedom, *real* freedom, recognizes the inherent worth of every human being. Freedom is the definition of equality actualized. Until each and every person is equally respected and safe regardless of color, creed, accent, IQ, bank balance, physical ability, vehicle they drive, job they have, who they sleep with, and whether they are on social security, we are not free.

In the eyes of the Divine, everyone is of sacred worth. Period.

BUILDING RELATIONSHIPS

It was hot. Well, *almost* hot by Appalachian standards. We had two volunteer crews on Claude and Margaret's house, which had little in the way of actual footers and a room where the floor had rotted out.

Together, the crews worked for five days to dig out the old footers, jacking up the house to get under the walls. We hand-mixed about three tons of concrete for new footers and set the house back down on solid cement blocks. At the same time, we tore out the floor of the room which would eventually be a handicap-accessible bathroom, broke out a huge rock in the middle of it (part of the mountain, I'm sure) with sledgehammers, and reframed the floor on top of the new footers.

If I do say so myself, we were awesome. We worked hard, worked well as a team, and got it all done. However, what I remember *most* about the week had nothing to do with work. It had to do with Claude and Margaret.

Margaret could probably qualify as older than the hills. For someone who had been living in a house that was falling down around her, she was still all smiles and warmth and flower print dresses. Her probably fifty-something-year-old son, Claude, in his plaid shirts and impish, *I'm-trouble* smiles liked to supervise and kid around with us throughout the week.

A couple of days at lunchtime, Dan, our fearless leader, brought out his guitar, and we sang songs and chit-chatted with Claude and Margaret while we ate soggy peanut butter and jelly sandwiches.

On our last day, we were dirty, sweaty, tired, and working hard to finish up when Claude brought out an ice-cold watermelon. I tell you, nothing has ever tasted so good, so sweet, so perfect. I didn't do too badly in the watermelon seed spitting contest either – go figure!

I guess, at the end of the day, what I'm trying to convey is that the most spiritual and valuable things that happened that week were the relationships we developed. It was about connecting in some natural human way with people who, at first glance, seemed very different from us. It was about recognizing how compassion, caring, and showing interest were just as important as, and maybe even more important than, fixing the house.

When we all come to the end of our lives, we may very well have forgotten people's names and exactly what happened and precisely what was said, but we'll remember how they made us feel.

SEEING DIFFERENTLY

I continue to be distressed and saddened by how polarized our country is over almost every little thing. I'm not talking about simple disagreements over an issue. I'm talking about angry, hateful, mean attacks on people who think differently – be it over wearing masks, opening the schools, racial issues, politics, religion, sexual orientation, or just about anything. We seem to have lost the ability to see one another as fellow human beings all trying to survive in this crazy, mixed-up world, all needing love and security, all needing to believe in our own worth.

Let me share a story with you from an old newsletter I once received . . .

Author and professor, John Westerhoff, told a story about a conference of Roman Catholics and Protestants he once led in Northern Ireland. While clergy and lay leaders of both groups came together to discuss theological issues, children from both communities were invited to join in a time of shared recreation. The hope, of course, was that people who spent time working and playing together would begin to let go of their fears and suspicions of one another.

Despite all the good intentions of the conference planners, Westerhoff confessed that the week was fraught with tension. Each day, he would begin by telling a Bible story about reconciliation. Yet, as the day's events wore on, antipathy and miscommunication continued to be a far more common reality than mutuality or understanding. He grew increasingly discouraged.

Finally, one morning, a Roman Catholic monk elected to sit on the floor with the children during the morning Bible story session. The story happened to be the one about the hemorrhaging woman who touched the hem of Jesus' garment and was healed. Westerhoff wrote about how after telling the story, he began to hear whispers coming from the other side of the room where the monk was sitting.

A little Protestant girl, looking at the man's strange garments, asked with mingled curiosity and urgency, "Can I touch you?"

"Of course," the monk replied.

"I'm scared," she answered. The monk looked puzzled, so she continued, "I'm scared because if my father knew I touched you, he might beat me."

The monk considered this carefully and then suggested that possibly her father wouldn't have to know. The little girl pondered this for a moment. Then, gathering courage, she reached out her finger and touched him. The whole room had fallen silent to watch the interchange.

The little girl looked at her finger. Then she looked back at the monk. "Nothing happened!" she exclaimed. Tears filled the eyes of more than one person in the room.

"Yes, it did," responded the monk. "You and I will never see the world the same again."

We desperately need to stop seeing the world in the same way.

It is only through risking "touching" each other – reaching out past our fears and defensiveness to get to know one another – that we will indeed begin to see past our differences. Only by seriously trying to imagine ourselves in another's shoes, we will begin to bridge the gap between fear, mistrust, and defensiveness and understanding and acceptance.

ACKNOWLEDGEMENTS

Long ago, in a time capsule compiled with my high school friends (all of whom are still in my life and are the best friends ever!), we predicted that I would write a book by the time I turned forty. Well, I missed that deadline by about fifteen years, but I am living proof that dreams do eventually come true. Thank you to those "old" friends who believed in me then and have stuck with me through all the ups and downs in life. You have been my rock for forty-plus years.

I cannot sufficiently express my gratitude to Sacred Journeys Spiritual Community, and especially a small group of people who believed enough in me and my message to risk starting our own church ten years ago. This has been an amazing journey of faith, learning, and growth. I am so very blessed to have a safe place to continue to push all of us to deeper and deeper levels of spirituality and service. You inspire me at every turn.

It was because of the gentle coaxing (and

occasional nagging) of a few Sacred Journeys members that I even considered turning these reflections into a book. To all of you, I know I hedged for a while, but thank you for your affirmations and persistence. However, without the constant encouragement and help from Bill Grimbol, I can say without a doubt that this book would not be. Thank you, Bill, for your friendship, your wisdom, your insight, your editing, and your irreverence.

To Marilyn Michna, who was a bright light with a wry sense of humor and a twinkle in her eye, thank you for your memorial gift to Sacred Journeys, which helped make this book possible.

To the staff, editors, and designers at Orange Hat Publishing | Ten16 Press, you have been a joy to work with. Thank you for helping put forth the best in me.

Often to their chagrin, my wonderful children have provided much sermon and reflection fodder over the years. Jordan, Sam, and Bryn, I love you all beyond measure, and I've used your stories because you have been the best teachers in my life. Thank you.

This summer, my daughter, Bryn, and I explored Sequoia and Yosemite National Parks. I mentioned that I wanted to take some pictures for the cover and inside sections of the book, and then I barely got my hands on the camera again. So, kudos to you, Bryn, for your creative eye and the beautiful pictures that enhance the messages in this book. I loved working with you.

And last, but never least, I am so grateful to my loving, walk-like-you'll-kick-someone's-ass wife. Julie, you have graciously read through all these pages more than once, you've given me the time and space to write and edit, and you've been supportive and encouraging through all my stress and anxiety about the process. Thank you for helping me achieve this dream and so many others. You are amazing, and I love you.

RESOURCES

BOOKS:

Brown, Brené – *Daring Greatly*
Brown, Brené – *The Gifts of Imperfection*
Cameron, Julia – *The Artist's Way*
Chawla, Navin – *Mother Teresa*
Chittester, Joan – *Called to Question*
Estes, Clarissa Pinkola – *Untying the Strong Woman*
Fulghum, Robert – *From Beginning to End*
Habegger, Larry; O'Reilly, James; and O'Reilly, Sean – *Stories to Live by*
Hawley, Jack – *The Bhagavad Gita*
Kidd, Sue Monk – *When the Heart Waits*
Kornfield, Jack – *A Path with Heart*
Larkin, Geri – *Stumbling Toward Enlightenment*
Nachmanovitch, Stephen – *The Art of Is*
Nepo, Mark – *Seven Thousand Ways to Listen*
Nepo, Mark – *The Exquisite Risk*
Nerburn, Kent – *Make Me an Instrument of Your Peace*

Newell, John Philip – *A New Harmony*

Norris, Kathleen – *Dakota*

Palmer, Parker – *On the Brink of Everything*

Palmer, Parker – *Let Your Life Speak*

Rupp, Joyce – *Open the Door*

Troeger, Thomas – *Sermon Sparks*

Whitcomb, Holly – *Seven Spiritual Gifts of Waiting*

INTERNET ARTICLES:

"The Art of Resilience" by Hara Estroff Marano - www.psychologytoday.com

"The Danger of Comparing Yourself to Others" - www.fs.blog

"How many hugs a day do we need to be happy?" - www.psychology-spot.com

"Hummingbird Migration" - www.hummingbirdcentral.com

"What are the Benefits of Hugging?" by Erica Cirino - www.healthline.com

CPSIA information can be obtained
at www.ICGtesting.com
Printed in the USA
LVHW010905020921
696503LV00004B/13